Generational Ties

Michel Robillard

Unless otherwise indicated, biblical quotations are taken from the *American King James Version*.

The names of the people in the examples quoted are fictitious, and sometimes two stories have been combined.

Original edition published in French under the title:
Les liens générationnels
Copyright © 2022 - Michel Robillard

English Version
Copyright © 2025 - Michel Robillard
All rights reserved.

It is illegal to reproduce any part of this book without the written permission of the author, except for brief quotations in scholarly works, books or magazines, with the mention. Any reproduction of this publication, by whatever means, will be considered an infringement of copyright.

Legal deposit - Bibliothèque nationale du Québec, 2025.
ISBN (print version): 978-2-9811011-5-0
(Original edition: ISBN (print version): 978-2-9811011-4-3)

*He has sent me to heal the brokenhearted,
to preach deliverance to the captives.*

Luke 4:18
The Bible

TABLE OF CONTENTS

Preface 7

Introduction 9

1 Original sin. 13
    The transmission of evil 19

2 The curse of sin. 25
    Three principles 29
    Biblical exemples. 36
    Iniquities 40
    Science and intergenerationnal 42
    Individualism that blinds us 46

3 Alliances. 51
    Human alliances 51
    A satanic agreement 53
    Divine covenants 56
    The transmission of hope 63
    Covenants and generational ties 67

4 Annoyed teeth 73
    An enigmatic metaphor 74
    Announcing a New Covenant 76
    Texts that make teeth gnash 79

5 Propitiation 81
    The effets of propitiation. 82
    Already, but not yet 84
    Asking to receive 87

6 The notion of links. 93
    Rights and gateways 94
    Fortresses. 96

    Tying and untying 97
    Devilish ties 103

7 Generational ties 109
    Curses that emprison 112
    A complex reality 116

8 Spirits and demons 119
    Knowledge of the enemy 120
    Demonization 122
    Generational spirits 126
    Discerning spirits 131
    Exorcism and baptism 133

9 The ministry of Jesus 137
    Jesus and the covenants 137
    Jesus and the root of evil 139
    Jesus and curses 139
    Jesus and demonized children 143
    Jesus and generational sins 145

10 The practice of liberation 149
    Checking the basics 155
    Reconstructing history 156
    Confessing and covering iniquity 157
    Undo curses 159
    Break generational ties 160
    Renounce alliances 161
    Drive out spirits 163
    Maintain liberation 166
    Preventive separation 169

Conclusion 171

Bibliography 177

Preface

From the outset, the author reassures us: this is a controversial subject, and he knows it! So, he puts us at ease right from the start. The sensitivity of the subject is perhaps the reason why there is so little documentation in French: hence the particular interest of this book.

There are many reasons why I appreciate and recommend Michel Robillard's book, which I would describe as rigorous and balanced overall. With solid biblical support and a wide-ranging examination of God's Word from cover to cover, he is able to explain to us simply and clearly various principles underlying a reality we must not overlook: certain sufferings experienced in the present may have their origins in past generations. At times, the author will scrutinize various concepts and biblical passages. In this way, he will satisfy the expectations of those who, like him, are concerned to examine the Scriptures and the teachings that can be drawn from them. He tackles head-on biblical passages that are controversial or used as arguments by those who would oppose the proposed approach. It also has the ability to refute the misuse of verses that might falsely support the concept of deliverance.

This book is a valuable contribution when, after many efforts to free ourselves from a difficulty, be it spiritual, psychological or even physical, we find ourselves at an impasse. Indeed, for the caregiver who feels he or she has examined the problem from every angle, without finding an answer, it's important to consider this question: could the origin come from the ancestors? And could the solution lie in breaking ties? This is what the author invites us to do, by proposing an approach that can become a source of liberation for the sufferer. However, he is wise to avoid the trap of "lumping everything together". Instead, he takes a holistic look at the experience of the person being helped, while avoiding hasty and indiscriminate conclusions. It's clear from reading this book that he knows how to take a whole range of factors into account. I agree with him that generational problems are never isolated; they should only form part of the intervention within the broader framework of support. This book is therefore an invaluable addition to the counsellor's toolbox. It will also be useful to the person being helped.

I'd also like to emphasize the care the author takes in insisting on the importance of making the right diagnosis and discerning the gateway at the origin of the hold the helpee is under. This is an essential aspect, likely to avoid clumsy approaches that could discredit the ministry of deliverance. Furthermore, it does not become simplistic by considering only the sin of the person being helped, but proposes a diversity of possibilities, including the traumas suffered. Likewise, he steers clear of any pretense of triumphant success, pointing out that, unfortunately, some people are not delivered. The gift of discernment is a precious asset. However, when this is not available to us, the author still encourages us to move forward in the process with God's wisdom and help. Finally, it's important to note that the focus is on the work of Jesus Christ on Calvary. Indeed, for any approach that claims to be Christian, the centrality of the Cross is inescapable. For everything is resolved in the person of Jesus!

We need to see Christ's disciples develop and use the tools that the Spirit distributes to the members of His Body, while recognizing our limitations and referring as needed. I have many years of experience in helping people. But this book has taught me a lot! For me, it's an invitation to be even more attentive to the generational dimension of helping others. May it be a source of inspiration for many!

René Laframboise
YWAM missionary,
counsellor and author

Introduction

Edward has just moved to a new town. He decides to attend a conference on deliverance. On the second day, a young girl approaches him and tells him she's had a dream. She believes it's about him. She sees that God wants to destroy the bad fruit of things that have happened in her family over four generations. Edward then asks the leader of a Christian group he attends for advice. She refers him to us. We begin a process of prayer for inner healing with him. We ask the Lord Jesus to teach us about the situation. He confirms the dream, showing us that Edward is indeed troubled by several generational ties that are causing him anger and sexual problems.

Julie came to us in prayer for inner healing. We had also met her father a few years earlier. As she prayed, Julie felt that her paternal grandmother was exercising emotional control over her. Julie's father had also told us that his mother was controlling him.

Mario and Sylvianne are particularly hard hit: illness, accidents, damage to the house. Similar problems arise in the families of Sylvianne's sisters and Mario's brothers. Here again, the Lord reveals that there are many generational ties caused by sins of violence and sexual abuse, and by witchcraft practices among the ancestors.

Carole is a Quebecker who asked for help because she felt that something was preventing her from making progress in her Christian life. We asked Jesus to show us the cause. Carole sees a village. As caregivers, we also listen in prayer, and see similar images at the same time. Describing the place, Carole recognizes it as the village where her grandmother lived in France. She's been there before. Then my wife asked her if she was a descendant of the Huguenots. Indeed, she is. Her ancestors were rejected and intimidated. Then the whole family became hostile to Catholics. Her parents decided to stop talking about religion and became lukewarm. We ask Carole to forgive her ancestors, and those who persecuted them. She also asks the Lord's forgiveness for her parents' indifference. The sessions that followed revealed a magnificent prophetic gift in Carole. Yet she knew nothing of prophecy, whereas Huguenots are renowned for it. We thought this gift lay dormant in her, blocked by generational sins.

Do these stories sound strange? But these people are real. And there are thousands of stories like these. However, people suffering from generational ties don't always know where to turn for help.

Inner healing prayer combines prayer and pastoral care. It relies on listening to God to access revelations that enable us to pray for body, soul and spirit, to bring healing and deliverance. All these aspects, which enable us to see the whole person, are rarely addressed by those working in the secular world. Yet there are situations that fall within the spiritual sphere, and sometimes they are generational in nature.

The generational perspective is one facet of prayer for inner healing. This book is dedicated to this very subject. Generational ties are caused by certain sins committed, or traumas suffered by ancestors, or curses that have struck an entire family. Evil spirits can also play a part in these dark events. The good news is that there are solutions.

The book you are about to read is part of a trio of books designed to publicize an approach to inner healing prayer that I have been developing over the last sixteen years. The first book gives a general introduction to this approach[1]. This first book should be of interest to many readers struggling with a variety of physical,

---

1   Robillard (Michel), *Espoir pour l'âme et l'esprit, le miracle de la guérison intérieure*, Québec, 2022, 124 p.

psychological or social problems, which, unwittingly or not, always have a spiritual dimension. It includes many testimonials and explanations of the miraculous aspects of divine intervention. There is also a training manual for people who would like to learn how to help others using this approach[2].

I composed the present volume because the amount of data to be transmitted on generational inheritance was too great to include in my other two publications. Moreover, there are few books dedicated to the study of generational ties in French and English-speaking circles. Several books devote a few pages to the subject, but this is insufficient to address all the theological and practical issues surrounding this controversial subject.

A controversial topic? Indeed, I find that Christian circles are divided on this issue. On the one hand, there are those who have been taught that generational ties cannot reach born-again Christians. On the other hand, there are those who believe in generational ties and demons because they have had experiences demonstrating these realities, but who have little theoretical knowledge on the subject. Those who don't believe in generational ties say that a believer cannot be punished for the sins of his ancestors. But have they really understood the biblical message? As for those who defend the existence of generational ties, they often quote passages irrelevant to the subject, or misapply them by taking them out of context, or using an allegorical interpretation. So their lack of theological rigor often contributes to discrediting the phenomenon of generational links, even when they report very striking testimonies.

I'm not a qualified exegete, but as I studied the subject, the Lord showed me a very clear direction. So, I begin my study with an analysis of original sin. I then demonstrate that the question of generational ties is analogous to this doctrine. In this way, I hope

---

[2] Robillard (Michel), *La prière de guérison intérieure – Manuel de formation*, Québec, 2022, 245 p.

to convince those who believe in the doctrine of original sin, but are hesitant to adopt a theology of generational ties. In this book, I have also studied several biblical texts in order to give those with experience of this reality the best possible support to explain it. My greatest wish is that the theological debates raised by this question of generational ties should not prevent us from bringing help to those who suffer, but that on the contrary, they should nourish our theoretical and practical knowledge. Besides, in the last chapter of this book, we conclude with a description of our pastoral approach, summarizing the tools we use to pray for the breaking of generational ties.

1
Original sin

It's generally accepted that we inherit genetic characteristics from our parents that influence our bodies as well as our way of thinking and perceiving. Genetically, we inherit beautiful things like artistic talent; but we also receive negative things like disease. What's more, we all have a cultural heritage, stemming from the community, including language and history. Finally, we have a heritage of values, beliefs and attitudes, transmitted in part by family upbringing. These three pathways – genetic, cultural and educational – contribute to our generational heritage.

There is a fourth, lesser-known path: spiritual inheritance. Some of these legacies are positive. For example, we sometimes see that the descendants of certain families where the Christian faith has been well established for several generations are exceptionally mature and morally beautiful[3]. Other spiritual legacies are harmful. These explain a number of phenomena that other modes of generational transmission are unable to elucidate, such as the increased prevalence in certain families of specific problems that are repeated from generation to generation, such as a series of premature deaths that far exceeds regional prevalence. These deleterious ancestral legacies come from three sources: sins, traumas and curses administered by generational spirits. Together, these harmful legacies weave what we call generational bonds. Unfortunately, the notion of generational ties is often met with skepticism, even in Christian circles.

---

[3] The new birth is not transmitted by blood ties (Jn 1.13), yet we are promised that the born-again will leave a beautiful inheritance to their children (Isa 59 :20-21). It is therefore possible for life in Christ to bequeath good legacies to offspring through education or even through certain genetic transformations (see the discussion on epigenetics in chapter 2).

Yet the concept of spiritual inheritance is akin to a doctrine universally recognized in the Church, that of original sin. That's why we'll begin our study with this subject. Indeed, a clear understanding of the nature and consequences of sin lays the foundation for any religion worthy of the name. This explains why there have been important debates on this subject in the history of Christianity. For example, as early as the 4th century, the Breton monk Pelage put forward the idea that God would have been unjust to subject all mankind to the consequences of Adam and Eve's sin. He therefore believed that human beings were not born sinners and had the capacity to resist sin. For him, sin was a social construct resulting from the bad example parents set for their children. Pelage's contemporary, the famous Augustine of Hippo, vehemently opposed these ideas. Later, in the 17th century, a similar debate took place between the followers of Arminius and Calvin. It also pitted theologians John Taylor and John Wesley against each other in the 18th century.

Wesley wrote extensively on original sin. His nine-volume treatise on the subject contains over 300 pages of textual exegesis alone. The reason Wesley was so interested in this subject, it seems, was that he anticipated the modern analysis of human failings later elaborated by Marx and Freud. Wesley was not in complete opposition to modern thinking on the modes of transmission of sin. He recognized the contribution of family and society to the genesis of neuroses, mores and political systems. But these vectors did not act without our participation, in his view[4]. Indeed, each person reacts differently when exposed to similar situations. Moreover, Wesley believed that these vectors were not sufficient to explain the transmission of sin. The presence of evil in society is linked to the invisible spiritual world to which the apostle Paul refers as the "mystery of iniquity" (2 Thess 2:7)[5]. Wesley thus refuted a frame of reference in which human beings

---

[4] Oden (Thomas C.), *John Wesley's teachings*, Vol. 1, Grand Rapids [MI], Zondervan, 2012, p. 219.
[5] *Ibid*, p. 202.

were solely conditioned by their environment. On the contrary, as the Church had professed for several centuries, he believed that God had allowed evil to enter the world because he wanted human beings to be free to make their own choices.

Wesley didn't just argue from the Bible. He also used common sense to convince his readers. Thus, he said, we can detect sin everywhere and at any time in the history of mankind. Empirical observation leads to the conclusion that sin is universal and perennial. Likewise, he appealed to the conscience of each individual to probe the human heart. Is there any man or woman who doesn't have the slightest hint of malice in him or her? The test of the Ten Commandments is pretty conclusive: love only God, have no other idols, do not use God's name in vain, keep the Sabbath, honor one's parents, do not commit murder, adultery, theft, lying, and do not desire what does not belong to you. Each of these categories can be very demanding. Theft, for example, is not just about big bank robberies or masterful fraud, but also about undeclared income or taking materials from the factory or office for our own personal use. Similarly, covetousness touches on the areas of sexuality, material goods and the status and privileges we envy in our fellow human beings. Any serious examination of conscience should lead us all to the conclusion that there is not a single righteous person on earth (Rom 3:10) and that God's law handed down to Moses does not serve to give us life, but to make us aware of sin (Rom 3:20). So we should avoid throwing stones at others, since we all deserve to be judged (Mt 7:1-5; Jn 8:7).

Despite the intervention of such a gifted intellectual as Wesley, it was becoming increasingly difficult in the 19th century to combat a fragmented conception of sin and defend the doctrine of original sin. Christian philosopher Soren Kierkegaard and physician Sigmund Freud defined the human problem as an ambivalence within the human. Karl Marx postulated that evil stems from socio-economic structure. Theologian and historian Richard F. Lovelace described the erosion of the understanding of sin, and the consequences that followed, as follows:

The Reformers perceived that fallen human nature was touched in every area by the deforming presence of original sin, the compulsive force operating behind individual acts of transgression. They believed that [...] apart from grace his best actions are still built upun the foundation of unbelief, and even his virtues are organiezed as weapons against the rule of God. [...]

In the eighteenth and nineteenth centuries this depth analysis of sin was abandoned by the growing rationalist movement [...] Gradually sin began to be difined in a way which seemed more rationally defensible: sins are conscious, voluntary acts of transgression against known laws. [...]

But the structure of sin in the human personality is something far more complicated than the isolated acts and toughts of deliberate disobedience commonly designated by the word. In its biblical definition, sin cannot be limited to isolated instances of patterns of wrongdoing; it is something much more akin to the psychological term complex: an organic network of compulsive attitudes, beliefs and behavior deeply rooted in our alienation from God. Sin originated in the darkening of the human mind and heart as man turned from the truth about God to embrace a lie about him and consequently a whole universe of lies about his creation. Sinful thoughts, words and deeds flow forth from this darkened heart automatically and compulsively, as water from a polluted fountain. "The LORD saw that the wickedness of man was great in the earth, and that every imagination of the thoughts of his heart was only evil continually" (Gen 6:5). This is echoad in Jesus' words: "Either make the tree good, and its fruit good; or make the tree bad, and its fruit bad; for the tree is known by its fruit. You brood of vipers! How can you speak good, when you are evil? For out of the abundance of the heart the mouth speaks. The good man out of his good treasure brings forth good, and the evil man out of his evil treasure brings forth evil" (Mt 12:33-35).

The human heart is now a reservoir of unconscious disordered motivation and response, of which unrenewed persons are unaware if left to themselves, for "the heart is deceitful above all things, and desperately corrupt; who can understand it?" (Jer 17:9). It is as if they were without mirrors and suffering from tunnel vision: they can see neither themselves clearly nor the great peripheral area around their immediate experience (God and supernatural reality). At the two most crucial loci of their understanding, their awareness of God and of themselves, they are almost in total darkness, although they may attempt to remedy this by framing false images of themselves and God. Paul describes this darkness of the unregenerate mind: "Now this I affirm and testify in the Lord, that you must no longer live as the Gentiles do, in the futility of their minds; they are hardened in their understanding, alienated from the life of God because of the ignorance that is in them, due to their hardness of heart" (Eph 4:17-18). The mechanism by which this unconscious reservoir of darkness is formed is identified in Rom 1:18-23 as repression of traumatic material, chiefly the truth about God and our condition, which the unregenerate constantly and dynamically 'hold down'[6].

I like this Lovelace' description of sin because it explains its nature using Scripture while engaging observations from psychology and history. This author demonstrates the seriousness of sin. Indeed, we must understand that it is more than a behavioral problem. The initial transgression of the first humans was inspired by a demon. Original sin has taken deep root, and the very root of human consciousness has been corrupted by the historic decision of our very first ancestors, Adam and Eve. Moreover, if we change the definition of sin to mere immoral acts, we affect the notion of salvation, for Jesus came to free us from our corrupt nature (Isa 53:6; Eph 2:5) and to redeem us from the power of evil spirits (Mk 10:45; 1 Tim 2:6; 1 Jn 3:8). Christ's aim was not to give us lessons in Christian morality!

---

6   Lovelace (Richard F.), *Dynamics of spiritual Life*, Downers Grove [IL], Intervarsity Press, 1979, pp. 86-94.

In the beginning, it was the decision not to trust God's word that led to the break in the relationship between God and man. Eve preferred to believe the serpent who suggested self-determination. This diabolical seducer instilled in her the idea that she and Adam would become like gods, able to define good and evil as they saw fit. But to do so, they had to question God's word and disobey him by eating of the fruit of the tree of the knowledge of good and evil. Eve therefore denied her Creator, preferring to follow Satan's path. Adam acquiesced, and God called him to account, considering him also responsible for original sin. This is why Paul says that "by one man sin entered into the world" (Rom 5:12). Adam and Eve strayed from God's goal through unbelief, pride and lust.

Satan is the father of lies (Jn 8:44). But what he said was partly true. It's true that, later on, humans were able to define good and evil as they pleased. But they didn't become as glorious as gods. Quite the contrary! The likeness they shared with God became tarnished (Gen 1:26). Their moral nature was corrupted. Sickness and death entered the world. All creation was affected (Rom 8:20-21). Sin polluted our conscience (Gen 3:1-6), and evil was perpetuated in the world through the activity of demons (Eph 2:1-3; 6:12).

Adam and Eve's sin had consequences. Because of the first humans, we lost our nobility, as well as the authority we had over all creation (Gen 1:28), for the seed of original sin contains within it the ability to reproduce vice and transgression in all humans (Rom 3:23). Humanity is now corrupt by nature (Eph 2:3). And that's what we're particularly interested in here: the transmissible nature of this original sin from generation to generation. Sin and death have passed to all humans, as this very revealing passage of Scripture states:

Why, as by one man sin entered into the world, and death by sin; and so death passed on all men, for that all have sinned.

Romans 5:12

The transmission of evil

This instructive passage underlines the fact that we all share in Adam and Eve's sin; we all sin and deserve death. But by what mechanism is this solidarity established? Theologians have wondered whether sin is transmitted through the body, the soul or the spirit. Above all, they have focused on the question of justice. How did God apply his justice to punish sin? What was exactly transmitted? Was the guilt of the first offence passed on to all mankind, in addition to the corruption of human nature?

Various ideas have been put forward to explain how original sin was transmitted to all mankind. One way of conceiving its transmission to subsequent generations is to say that Adam represented all humans when he made his covenant with God. Therefore, by disobeying God, he would have dragged us all down with him in his fall. This concept, known as "federalism", implies that Adam's guilt is passed on to all humans. Theologian Wayne Grudem defends this idea based on the tense of the verb *hèmarton* used in Romans 5:12 : "all have sinned". He says that this aorist indicative verb in the historical narrative indicates a completed past action.

> Here Paul is saying that something happened and was completed in the past, namely, that "all men sinned". But it was not true that all men had actually committed sinful actions at the time that Paul was writing, because some had not even been born yet, and many others had died in infancy before committing any conscious acts of sin. So Paul must be meaning that when Adam sinned, God considered it true that all men sinned in Adam[7].

This idea that Adam represented all humanity is also supported by the fact that the apostle Paul holds Adam responsible for original sin. Yet it was Eve who committed this sin. Adam

---

7   Grudem (Wayne), *Systematic Theology*, Grand Rapids [MI], Zondervan, 1994, note 9, p. 494.

merely agreed to it and then participated in it. Here, Paul breaks completely with the teaching of the rabbis, who never missed an opportunity to hold women responsible for sin and to emphasize the inferior nature of their sex.

Grudem thus asserts that Adam's guilt is imputed to us because we are represented in him. He believes that both guilt and corruption were transmitted to mankind through original sin[8]. Similarly, the eminent Calvinist theologian Charles Hodge, who directed Princeton Theological Seminary, N.J., from 1851 to 1878, describes the theology of federalism in these words:

> No fact in history is plainer than that children bear the iniquities of their fathers. They suffer from their sins. There must be a reason for this; and a reason founded in the very constitution of our nature. But there was something peculiar in the case of Adam. Over and beyond this natural relation which exist between a man and his posterity, there was a special divine constitution by which he was appointed the head and representative of his whole race[9].

Federalism is a logical deduction that has the advantage of explaining the transmission of sin. However, a careful reading of Romans 5:12 shows us that this text does not expose the transmission of guilt with as much clarity as these theologians assert. Indeed, Paul says that sin entered the world because of Adam, and that this resulted in death for all humans. However, Paul does not clearly mention that guilt was also passed on. In fact, the apostle closes Romans 5:12 by mentioning a third theological proposition which states, in black and white, that if corruption has spread to all men, it is "because all have sinned". If sin had been transmitted by representation, we would have expected Paul to state that the transmission of moral corruption to humans took

---

8   *Ibid*, pp. 494-496.
9   Hodge (Charles), *Systematic Theology*, Vol. 2, [n.l.], Hendrickson Publishers, 2003, p. 197.

place because they inherited the guilt of original sin. But Paul does not say this. He merely states that humans are guilty of their own participation in sin, not of original sin by association with Adam. So it seems to me that Paul's last proposition contradicts rather than supports the theology of federalism.

Then there's the argument about the verb *hèmarton*. Grudem observes that the word "all" is incompatible with the past tense of the verb, since not all humans have yet been born. He postulates that this "all" also designates future humans, and then deduces that the unborn are sinners, by representation, before they themselves have sinned. But we would also be faithful to the text if we understood that Paul is simply noting here that "all" men who have lived to him have been sinners in the past, without exception. It's an empirical fact, as Wesley would say. Moreover, the rest of the text, just two verses later, makes it clear that Paul is not talking about the future:

> *Nevertheless death reigned from Adam to Moses,*
> *even over them that had not sinned*
> *after the similitude of Adam's transgression, [...]*
>
> Romans 5:14

Rather, Paul notes that the men who lived in the past – from Adam to Moses – were all mortal, even if they themselves did not commit the original sin. He's not talking about the future. What's more, he expressly states that they did not commit Adam's fault. If Paul had had in mind that all are guilty in Adam, he would have had a great opportunity to say so here. We would have expected something like, "Death reigned from Adam until Moses, because united in Adam's seed, humans committed the transgression in him and are therefore guilty," but that's not what we read. Paul is only talking about the consequences for all mankind. He's talking about the inheritance of a sinful state for every man; a state that has resulted in death for all who have lived up to it. We became mortal and separated from God even before we committed any sin. This description always refers to the corruption of our nature and the curses of original sin. Paul does not mention the guilt of our descendants.

Federalists say that there can be no consequences without first being at fault. But where does this principle come from? The Bible clearly states in Romans 8 that all creation inherits corruption. Yet it is not guilty of anything! What's more, Jesus Christ himself is the model of a guiltless man who nevertheless bore many of the consequences of Adam's fall (suffering, temptation, death)[10]. Experience also shows us that we can suffer harm as a result of something we didn't do! To sum up, I believe Paul affirms two consequences of original sin: we became mortal and sinful because of Adam. The apostle does not, however, speak of any inheritance of Adam's guilt[11].

Later on, we'll look at a number of passages that say the same thing. First, I'd like to comment on a text often used by Federalists. 1 Corinthians 15:21-22 states that death entered the world "through" (διά) Adam, and that all die "in" (ἐν) Adam. The word "through" underlines the relationship between cause and effect; "in" underlines the solidarity of all humanity. Some Federalists deduce from this that we were all represented in him, and therefore guilty. However, Paul does not say this. He says only that we suffer the consequence of sin, which is death, through and in Adam. We die because of Adam, and we share in his death by inheriting this curse. There is nothing here to show that we are punished with Adam, for Adam's fault. Our guilt comes from the fact that we commit sins, in our turn, because of the corrupt

---

10 Karl Barth presents Jesus as fully human. Although free from sin, Christ had to be mortal in order to die in our place. Yet he overcame death. Allen, (Michael), *Karl Barth's church Dogmatics - an introduction and reader*, London and New-York, T & T Clarck, 2012, pp. 143-144, notes 3 and 4.
11 Note that this position is not Pelagian, for Pelagius went much further in asserting that we did not inherit the moral corruption of sin as a consequence of Adam's sin. Now, I believe that sin is deeply rooted in us, as Lovelace has described.

nature we inherit. It doesn't come from original sin, because we didn't commit it.

Why is it so important to distinguish between inheriting only the tendency to commit sin and inheriting the guilt of original sin as well? After all, we are sinners and mortals in both cases! This distinction is essential, as it sheds light on our understanding of generational ties, since these ties are also the consequences of previous events, but are not linked to the guilt of those who inherit them.

The idea that all humans suffer the consequences of original sin, without inheriting Adam's guilt, finds support in theologians such as Bruce R. Marino and Myer Pearlman.

> All humanity, in some sense, is united or bound to Adam as a single entity (because of him, all people are outside the blessedness of Eden; Rom 5:12-21; 1 Cor 15:21-22)[12].

> The effect of the fall was so deep-seated in human nature that Adam, as the father of the race, passed on to his descendants a tendency or bias to sin. Psalm 51:5. This spiritual and moral handicap under which all men are born is known as original sin. […] This moral condition of the soul is described in many ways: all have sinned (Rom 3:9); all are under the curse (Gal 3:10); […] the mental and moral nature is corrupt (Gen 6:5,12; 8:21; Rom 1:19-31); […] the sinner is a slave of sin (Rom 6:17; 7.5); is controlled by the prince of the power of the air (Eph 2:2) […][13].

Original sin is therefore the historical fact of the disobedience of the first human beings, from which the universal transmission

---

12 Marino (Bruce R.), « The Origin, Nature, and Consequences of Sin », in : Horton (Stanley M.) *Systematic Theology*, Springfield [MI], Gospel Publishing House, 2000, p. 261.
13 Pearlman (Myer), *Knowing the Doctrines of the Bible*, Springfield [MI], Gospel Publishing House, 2018, pp. 134-135.

of our sinful nature and mortal status ensued[14]. This doctrine states that we are demoted to a condition inferior to our original design. Wesley spoke of original sin as a mold in which all sins are formed.

> Original sin is the first form of sin in human history that dates back to the primordial beginning of the human story. That sin is original which is the archetype of subsequent sin, derivative from the first sin, and being configured from the human fallen condition becomes the formative pattern other sins in history[15].

From this form of sin flow all the other sins: doubting the veracity of God's Word, rebellion, independent emancipation from God, arrogance in defining good and evil, pride in seeking to be like gods, creature worship. The mold of original sin has set the course of world history. The disposition to commit sin has engendered ever more sins and curses (disease, death, suffering, etc.) from generation to generation.

---

14 The immortality of Adam and Eve at the moment of creation is not specifically mentioned in the Genesis account. We can, however, deduce it from the fact that God told them they would die if they ate from the tree of the knowledge of good and evil, and from the fact that the apostle Paul says that death entered the world the moment they sinned.

15 Oden (Thomas C.), *op. cit.*, pp. 212-213.

2
The curse of sin

In making the Adamic covenant, God had warned the first man of the consequences of breaking it.

And the LORD God commanded the man, saying,
Of every tree of the garden you may freely eat:
But of the tree of the knowledge of good and evil,
you shall not eat of it:
for in the day that you eat thereof you shall surely die.

Genesis 2:16-17

Let's note an important point right away: God is good. Although He is just and can chastise, He rarely does so, for He is "merciful and gracious, slow to anger, abounding in lovingkindness and faithfulness" (Ex 34:6). He doesn't take pleasure in sending us curses. Moreover, "he cannot be tempted by evil" (Jas 1:13). I therefore believe that the majority of curses reported in the Bible are, in fact, the consequences of human choices. In short, evil comes into play when humans distance themselves from God. When God says "the day you do this... you will die", he's not making a malicious threat, but warning of the consequences of turning away from the Creator, the source of life, and joining forces with the evil one, the source of death. So God instructs man realistically.

We see the results of Adam and Eve's disobedience in the Genesis story. When sin was consumed, the man and woman felt vulnerable and began to hide (Gen 3:7-8). They accused each other (Gen 3:12). Then, driven out of paradise, they became mortal, as predicted in Genesis 3:19. It's interesting to see in the text what justifies the expulsion from the Edenic garden. It was necessary to prevent humans affected by evil from taking of the tree of life and thus living eternally in this fallen state (Gen 3:22). God's act of justice was therefore preventive in scope, aimed at the good of mankind and its destiny, for God already had a plan to redeem mankind. At the time, it was necessary to limit the damage. The expulsion was not primarily a punishment, as many have assumed. Above all, the divine decree was intended to put history on hold until the Redeemer came and access to paradise was once again possible.

In addition to death, other curses have befallen man and woman as a result of original sin.

To the woman he said,
I will greatly multiply your sorrow and your conception;
in sorrow you shall bring forth children;
and your desire shall be to your husband,
and he shall rule over you.

And to Adam he said,
Because you have listened to the voice of your wife,
and have eaten of the tree, of which I commanded you, saying,
You shall not eat of it: cursed is the ground for your sake;
in sorrow shall you eat of it all the days of your life;
Thorns also and thistles shall it bring forth to you;
and you shall eat the herb of the field;
In the sweat of your face shall you eat bread,
till you return to the ground; for out of it were you taken:
for dust you are, and to dust shall you return.

Genesis 3:16-19

Theologian Wayne Grudem makes a relevant remark about this:
> In the punishments God gave to Adam and Eve, he did not introduce new roles or functions, but simply introduced pain and distortion into the functions they previously had[16].

---
16 Grudem (Wayne), *op. cit.*, p. 463.

In the creation order, women are biologically designed to bear children. It is therefore she who will suffer the curse in this role, is destined for her by nature. Man, on the other hand, will suffer in his role as gardener, which he inherited when he sealed his covenant with God. And through him, all creation will be cursed. "For the creature was made subject to vanity [*mataiotes*[17]] – not willingly, but by reason of him who has subjected it" (Rom 8:20). Most exegetes link this corruption to the curse of the earth, which stems from the sin described in Genesis 3:17-18[18].

Note that the words "sorrow" which express the difficulties of the woman and the man in Genesis 3:16 and 17 are translations of a single word (*itsabon*) which is not the usual word for physical pain. The meaning of this word would rather involve the idea of more laborious work. The consequences of sin would therefore be very similar for man and woman. As Grudem mentioned, all human activities already created are affected, both at home and outside the family nucleus.

Archaeologist and biblical historian Carol Meyers goes even further. According to her, the woman, being called to collaborate with the man (Gen 1:27-28), would have difficulties similar to those of the man for all tasks related to his work, and not only to give birth or to accomplish domestic tasks[19]. If we pursue this line of reasoning, the man who takes part in domestic tasks and the education of his children would also find this work more laborious than it was before original sin. So, in this sharing of tasks, both men and women experience the consequences of sin.

---

17 This Greek word means perversity, fragility. The French Bible *Le Semeur* translates it as "power of fragility". Plants and animals have inherited disease and death. Man causes the fragility of the ecosystem. All this began in Eden and continues day after day (Rom 5 :12).

18 Fee (Gordon), *God's Empowering Presence – The Holy Spirit in the Letters of Paul*, Grand Rapids [MI], Baker Academics, 1994, pp. 570-571 et note 292.

19 Hess (Richard S.), « Equality With and Without Innocence », in Pierce (R.W.), Groothuis (R.M.), Fee (G.D.), *Discovering Biblical Equality*, Downers Grove [IL], InterVarsity Press, 2005, p. 90.

This Genesis text also describes a direct consequence on the relationship between man and woman. The woman's desires are directed toward her husband, but he will rule over her. If we limit the meaning of the word *itsabon* to childbirth, we are then inclined to link the notion of desire to sexual life. The interpretation that follows is that the woman is sentimental and seeks the affection of a man, even if he may be violent towards her. However, a more careful analysis of the original Hebrew indicates that the word translated as "desire" (*teshûqäh*) generally evokes a craving for power, not sexual or romantic desire. Furthermore, the same phrase is repeated in Genesis 4:7 where six words are identical, which is highly significant linguistically. Now, in Genesis 4, sin is depicted as a crouching animal, ready to pounce on Cain. The "desire" (*teshûqäh*) of this sin-figured animal is to kill him, which is far from romantic! Thus, the word *teshûqäh* denotes aggressive conquest. Consequently, if we read the text of Genesis 3:16 in light of Genesis 4:7, the woman's goal since the fall would be to usurp male power[20]. This rebellious woman would observe and await the opportunity to overthrow the authority given to man by the Creator. She seeks conflict with him and rejects his leadership. Collaboration is broken. The woman no longer wants to be under the man's wing, as a joyful and willing helper similar to him (Gen 2:18), to fulfill with him the mission entrusted by the Creator. But now, the man, having become a sinner like his wife, reacts by accentuating his power. He will crush any rebellion. He will dominate the woman and abuse his strength. From being a protector, he will become a tyrant. He will demand submission. She will reluctantly adopt a servile attitude. Thus, sin has led to a power struggle.

We must be aware that this struggle does not stem from creation. It is the consequence of sin. God's original plan is a healthy "submission" of the woman, who willingly places herself

---

20 Grudem (Wayne), op. cit., p. 463. Grudem quotes Susan T. Foh's study: *What is Woman's Desire?* Westminster Theological Journal, vol. 37 (1975), pp. 376-383.

"under the mission[21]" entrusted to man. In the image of the Trinitarian relationship Father-Son-Spirit, Genesis 1, Genesis 2, and 1 Corinthians 11 present woman as a trustworthy partner. She is the glory of man and collaborates with him to steward this world. Submission, therefore, did not begin with the intrusion of sin. On the contrary, domination and power struggles were introduced into the world at the time of the fall. Sin has distorted this voluntary and joyful submission of woman, just as it has tarnished the leadership of man and most human capacities. Therefore, as Christians, we must combat evil by discerning and denouncing situations of abuse and sexism. At the same time, we must also encourage good male leadership and healthy collaboration between men and women in order to rediscover God's original plan.

Finally, note that in pronouncing the curses in the passages we have just read, God does not address Adam and Eve by their proper names. He speaks to them using generic terms. Thus, God pronounces a sentence upon all of humanity. All will suffer the consequences of original sin. This does not mean that humans are collectively guilty of the original sin through the Adamic covenant. This text simply underscores that the consequences of the sin of two individuals fall upon all men and all women.

Three principles

So far, three principles emerge from what we have said:
1. Adam and Eve are guilty of original sin, but not their descendants (humanity).
2. Their descendants have inherited a tendency to sin.
3. Their descendants have inherited curses that affect:
    a. the body (becoming mortal, subject to disease);
    b. activities (difficulties in work and family);
    c. relationships (power struggles);
    d. the environment (the whole creation deteriorates).

---

21 This is the etymology of the word "submission".

These principles now determine the condition of humanity and the system in which we live. They are forces more powerful than our will (Rom 7:22-23). Now, if these facts are well established, we have still not explained how the tendency to sin is transmitted. The federalism model had the advantage of justifying this transmission: we were all guilty in Adam; therefore, we all suffered the curses. But we reject this model. By what process will we now explain the dissemination of the consequences of sin? This question is closely related to the inquiry concerning the source of the human soul at the moment of birth. Tertullian, one of the early theologians of the Church, proposes a model that was later named traducianism.

> Tertullian believed that souls perpetuate themselves by way of generation, per traducem, and that as a result, the striking resemblance often observed between the character of children and that of their parents arises. He concluded that the corruption produced by the first sin in Adam had been hereditarily transmitted through generation to his descendants, so that there is in souls, by virtue of their origin, ex originis vitio, a kind of natural evil, malum, quodummodo naturale. This is the first germ of the doctrine of original sin, although Tertullian is still far from supposing that this sin renders humans incapable of any kind of good. On the contrary, he insists, as strongly as other teachers of his time, on the continuity of human freedom. He even thinks much less of an imputation of Adam's sin, since he explicitly states that the child, from the earliest age, is still innocent[22].

Tertullian provides us here with a conceptual model that takes into account biblical facts. Humanity is not born guilty – which is, however, the logical deduction of federalism – but inherits, through natural means (via the soul or genetics), a tendency to

---

22 [On Line] http://www.cosmovisions.com/Traducianisme.htm (June 27, 2021).

sin that is passed down from generation to generation. Following the logic of this model, it is not only the consequences of Adam and Eve's sin that can be transmitted, but also those of the sins of a succession of ancestors. Each time one of them commits a sin, it can have consequences for their descendants. Indeed, the intergenerational transmission of the tendency to sin and the transfer of the consequences of these sins occur in the same way for both the original sin and subsequent sins. The only difference is that we express things on a different scale. Paul looked through the telescope and saw that the first sin would eventually contaminate the whole planet. But we can also examine things one link at a time, and observe them on a smaller scale. To better understand, imagine you are an astronaut orbiting the Earth in a space capsule. From there, you can distinguish dense forest areas and differentiate them from water or desert spaces. But you cannot tell if you see deciduous or coniferous trees. For that, you would need to fly in a plane. Then you could see the type of trees that make up each forest. However, with this aerial view, you still wouldn't know if these trees are healthy or not. It is only by walking down into the forest that you could observe each tree up close.

The same goes for the subject we are discussing. Our observation of the original sin and curses resulting from the behavior of Adam and Eve is comparable to the astronaut's view of the planet. It gives us a view of humanity's universal and perpetual problem. If we look closer, we can observe that the prevalence of sins and generational ties is stronger in some families than in others. This is the equivalent of observing the forest from a plane. Finally, it is only by working on an individual basis that we can see what influence various ties have had on a person's life, as each person reacts differently, even in the presence of common factors. This individualized approach is equivalent to a close observation in the forest.

The concept of generational ties has the advantage of explaining the observed reality. Indeed, humans do not all commit the same sins. Humanity is like a great mosaic. There is a diversity of issues on each branch of humanity's genealogical tree. This notion is known in genetics. It also applies in the psychosocial and spiritual domains. Moreover, each individual can either submit to or combat the wrong tendencies that affect them. John Wesley, who lived at the time of the birth of modern science, described it this way:

> Your sin can affect me; my sin can affect my grandchildren; my grandfather's sin can affect me in ways difficult to understand exhaustively, yet to some degree subject to empirical analysis. These causal chains are not wholly mysterious or beyond inquiry, yet there remains a stubborn element of the mystery of iniquity in all human freedom, since these causal chains are often hidden in the complex history of freedom's outcomes. […] Social processes obviously transfer sin but not without our willing it. Each of us reinforces and relives the history of Adam and Eve's fallenness[23].

All this, as our three main principles summarize, is found in many passages of the Bible. But before we go further, let's open a parenthesis here for readers who may be less familiar with the Holy Scriptures. The Word of God cannot contradict itself because although the books of the Bible were written by different authors, in different eras, these texts are inspired by the Lord. Therefore, the teachings found in this great library are consistent with each other. This does not mean that the various authors were merely secretaries copying audible words from God. They composed their texts in collaboration with Him. They were aware that they had to accurately report the revelations they had received, and God sovereignly watched over each of their words. Moreover, Jesus attached importance to the smallest stroke of the letter of

---

23 Oden (Thomas C.), *op. cit.*, pp. 218-219.

the Scriptures (Mt 5:18; Lk 16:17). As for Paul, he affirmed that all Scripture is inspired (2 Tim 3:16). He also said: *Which things also we speak, not in the words which man's wisdom teaches, but which the Holy Ghost teaches; comparing spiritual things with spiritual*[24]. Here, the word *logos* is translated as 'words'. It is sometimes translated as 'speech', 'language', or 'terms'. Several theologians therefore believe that even the terminology used is inspired. According to them, it is not just the concept that is inspired.

Since the Bible is consistent and precise in its affirmations, it is not surprising that we find the three principles I speak of under the pen of various authors in contexts other than teaching on original sin. For example, we see in the book of Deuteronomy (one of the books of the Mosaic law) two texts that speak of the inheritance of the consequences of sin. First, it is said that God punishes the iniquity of the fathers on the children.

> *[...] For I the LORD your God am a jealous God, visiting the iniquity of the fathers on the children to the third and fourth generation of them that hate me,*
>
> Deuteronomy 5:9

Then, Moses, the author of this book (Deut 1:1), also writes that each will be condemned for their own sins.

> *The fathers shall not be put to death for the children, neither shall the children be put to death for the fathers: every man shall be put to death for his own sin.*
>
> Deuteronomy 24:16

How do we reconcile these two passages? We can reconcile them if we understand that the 'punishment' for the sins of the ancestors is that they suffer the consequences, not that they are

---

24 1 Corinthiens 2:13.

morally guilty of them (Deut 5). Therefore, since the descendants are not guilty of the faults of the ancestors, sons and daughters cannot be handed over to human justice as if they themselves had committed these sins. Only the guilty will be (Deut 24).

If we do not understand the principles we have discussed, we will see a contradiction in Moses' words here. Such a contradiction could also be perceived in the writings of the prophet Jeremiah, who expresses these two apparently contradictory realities in one and the same passage of the Scriptures.

You show loving kindness to thousands, and recompense the iniquity of the fathers into the bosom of their children after them: the Great, the Mighty God, the LORD of hosts, is his name, Great in counsel, and mighty in work: for your eyes are open on all the ways of the sons of men: to give every one according to his ways, and according to the fruit of his doings:

Jeremiah 32:18-19

How can Jeremiah affirm on one hand that God punishes the iniquity of the fathers in the bosom of their children and then say just after that He renders to each according to their ways? The only solution is that there is no contradiction in the eyes of this author. This text, just like those of Moses in Deuteronomy, can only be understood in light of the principles we have deduced from our reading of Genesis and chapter 5 of Romans: only the ancestors are guilty, but the descendants suffer the consequences.

Several theologians are very perplexed by these texts because they do not use the right principles to interpret them. For example, an internet user asks theologian John Piper how to reconcile the passages that say that the descendants suffer the fault of the fathers (Ex 20:5-6; 34:6-7; Lev 26:39) and those that teach that each must pay for their own sin (Deut 24:16; 2 Kgs 14:6)[25]. Piper tries to solve the dilemma by affirming that 'the sins of the fathers are punished on the sons when they become the sins of the children.' Note firstly that this position diverges even further from the doctrine of federalism than I do. Indeed, federalism stipulates that children inherit the corruption (tendency to sin and curses) and the guilt of Adam and Eve. I adopt the position that they only inherit the two aspects of corruption (curses and tendency to sin), and not their guilt. Piper here only accepts that we have inherited the tendency to sin. He admits that we do not inherit the guilt of the ancestors, and he struggles to believe that we can inherit curses for the faults committed by our fathers. That's why he connects the consequences to the sins of the descendants themselves.

However, this is not what these texts say. They literally declare that we have a God 'who punishes the iniquity of the fathers on the children.' Moses does not tell us here that God punishes the children only if they also commit the same sins. The prophet Isaiah speaks similarly:

> *Your first father has sinned,*
> *and your teachers have transgressed against me*[26].
> *Therefore I have profaned the princes of the sanctuary,*
> *and have given Jacob to the curse, and Israel to reproaches.*
>
> Isaiah 43:27-28

And again, the historians who wrote the books of Kings, when they speak of Josiah and his father Manasseh, affirm that the people are punished because of the sins of their ancestors. The good deeds of the son did not cancel the curses resulting from the horrors committed by the father (2 Kgs 21:11-12; 23:26; 24:4).

---

25 [On line] « Questions et rép. À John Piper », https://www.reveniralevangile.com/ma-vie-peut-elle-etre-marquee-par-des-peches-des-sorts-ou-des-maledictions-generationnels/, (July 2020).

26 We're talking here about Adam's original sin and the sins of the Doctors of the Law, whose task it was to act as intermediaries between God and man.

And it took another four generations, that of the great-grandsons of Manasseh, before God punished the whole people by deporting them to Babylon.

> *And like to him was there no king before him,*
> *that turned to the LORD with all his heart, and with all his soul,*
> *and with all his might, according to all the law of Moses;*
> *neither after him arose there any like him.*
> *Notwithstanding the LORD turned not*
> *from the fierceness of his great wrath,*
> *with which his anger was kindled against Judah,*
> *because of all the provocations*
> *that Manasseh had provoked him with.*
>
> 2 Kings 23:25-26

Biblical exemples

The Bible doesn't just teach us in statements and laws. It also recounts several lived experiences that demonstrate the principles of intergenerational transmission of curses related to certain sins. For example, it tells the story of Cain, who killed Abel, and who will experience more opposition than his parents did in cultivating the land. He will fear being killed, and his descendants will also inherit wandering and fear (Gen 4:10-14). They will be violent as their patriarch was (Gen 4:23-24). Similarly, the descendants of Jehu will pay for all the bloodshed he caused (Hos 1:4). As for King David, he wanted to clarify that he did not order the murder of Abner. It was his army commander Joab who set a trap for the enemy general Abner and who had to suffer the consequences of this murder. Furthermore, David specifies that Joab's descendants are targeted by the curse.

> *[…] I and my kingdom are guiltless before the LORD for ever*
> *from the blood of Abner the son of Ner:*
> *Let it rest on the head of Joab, and on all his father's house;*
> *and let there not fail from the house of Joab one that has an issue,*

> *or that is a leper, or that leans on a staff,*
> *or that falls on the sword, or that lacks bread.*
>
> 2 Samuel 3:28-29

Finally, the generation that rejected Jesus will not only pay for crucifying Him but also for all the blood of the prophets shed before (Mt 23:35). Indeed, it is to absolve himself from the curse of shedding innocent blood that Pilate washes his hands (Mt 27:24). All these accounts show that the shedding of blood in the murder of an innocent demands vengeance and constitutes a curse for posterity.

Murder is not the only sin that brings a curse on descendants. The negligence of Eli, the priest who did not correct his sons as he should have, will cause the death of his children and the definitive interruption of the priesthood privilege for all his descendants (1 Sam 2:29-34; 3:13-14). Jeroboam's idolatry will trigger a curse on his family (1 Kgs 14:9-11). The constant dissatisfaction and rebellion of the Israelites in the wilderness would have led God to exterminate them several times if not for Moses' intercession. In His mercy, God forgave His people (Num 14:20), thus removing their guilt. Nevertheless, in verses 21 to 23, we see that no Israelite from this rebellious generation will be able to enter the promised land. Their incessant criticism will have consequences even if they are forgiven.

The story of King David also shows that the tendency to violence and sexual sins can be passed on to descendants. This hero is nevertheless a man after God's own heart (1 Sam 13:14). However, he commits the sin of coveting Bathsheba, and even goes so far as to have her husband Uriah killed in order to take her as his wife. After committing adultery and rape[27], she becomes pregnant from this illegitimate union. The conceived child dies. David then repents dramatically, but it still has consequences. His sons will imitate his bad sexual behavior and his violence. The prophet Nathan also predicts this:

---

27 Indeed, as the king's subject, Bath-Sheba could not refuse him this favor, which became an abuse of power.

> *Now therefore the sword shall never depart from your house;*
> *because you have despised me, and have taken the wife*
> *of Uriah the Hittite to be your wife.*
> *Thus said the LORD,*
> *Behold, I will raise up evil against you out of your own house,*
> *and I will take your wives before your eyes,*
> *and give them to your neighbor,*
> *and he shall lie with your wives in the sight of this sun.*
> *For you did it secretly:*
> *but I will do this thing before all Israel, and before the sun.*
>
> 2 Samuel 12:10-12

This prophecy is fulfilled. Amnon, David's firstborn, rapes his half-sister Tamar, Maacah's daughter. His third son, Absalom, also born to Maacah, kills Amnon to avenge his sister. He then has to flee. David delays reconciliation with him, and Absalom foments a rebellion against his father. Taking power, this rebellious son receives advice from Ahithophel, a master strategist: " Go in to your father's concubines, which he has left to keep the house; and all Israel shall hear that you are abhorred of your father: then shall the hands of all that are with you be strong (2 Sam 16:21)." So, Absalom pitches a tent on the palace roof and sleeps with his father's concubines, thus fulfilling the curse announced[28] by Nathan (2 Sam 16:22). Shortly after, David's army regains power. Absalom dies by Joab's hand. However, David mourns the death of his son. The people are surprised. Shouldn't David be grateful to those who help him regain power? The text does not explain David's behavior. However, we can presume that the love he felt for his son was not the only cause of his tears. It is possible that

---

28 I'm not using the word "pronounced" here, although it would be linguistically appropriate. I want to emphasize what we explained at the beginning of the chapter: God wishes happiness, not misfortune. He announces the consequences of disobedience, but it breaks his heart. In the same way, the prophet may announce curses, but it is not with a good heart that he distributes misfortune, as a sorcerer would do when practicing black magic.

David remembered Nathan's prophecy and realized that all these misfortunes were linked to his own sin.

And it doesn't stop there. David grows old. Adonijah, David's fourth son, born to Haggith, would like to take his place. But David decides it will be Solomon, Bathsheba's son, who will become king. However, as soon as he is in power, Solomon commits a murderous act against his family. He has his half-brother Adonijah killed to secure his position (1 Kgs 2:24-25). He will then have many wives who lead him to foreign gods, displeasing the Lord (1 Kgs 11:6-8). Then comes the third generation. Rehoboam succeeds his father Solomon, and the kingdom is divided because of his pride. Ten of the twelve tribes of Israel follow King Jeroboam. Only two tribes remain loyal to Rehoboam (1 Kgs 12). Many wars and bloodshed will result from this schism.

Some may see only coincidences in these details, or attribute the various sins committed by David's family to generally sinful human nature. But we observe the specific nature of the sins committed. These sins are linked to violence and sexuality, like David's initial fault. Moreover, the prophet Nathan established a very clear link between David's sin and the consequences it would have for his house, namely his descendants. The pronounced curse concerns precisely violence and sexuality. Finally, such a concentration of these sins is relatively exceptional in the entirety of biblical accounts. Other texts report different sins, but not all families seem to have been as violent and sexually perverse as David's family. We may also wonder if David himself had inherited these tendencies from his ancestors. He said, "Behold, I was shaped in iniquity; and in sin did my mother conceive me." (Ps 51:5). Several biblical commentaries on this passage mention that David's father, Jesse of Bethlehem, had conceived him in adultery, with a mother who was not his wife. Furthermore, his great-great-grandmother was Rahab, the Canaanite prostitute who had helped the Israelites seize Jericho (Josh 2:1; Mt 1:5).

Iniquities

A particular Hebrew word also enriches our teaching on generational links. The word *awvon*, translated into English as "iniquity," is often used in the Old Testament to refer to the sins of ancestors that have consequences for their descendants. However, the word *awvon* is not specific; it can also refer to our own faults. For example, Moses prophesies Israel's disobedience using this same word for both personal faults and those of their fathers:

> *And they that are left of you shall pine away*
> *in their iniquity in your enemies' lands;*
> *and also in the iniquities of their fathers*
> *shall they pine away with them.*
> *If they shall confess their iniquity,*
> *and the iniquity of their fathers, [...]*
>
> Leviticus 26:39-40

Even though Moses only uses the word *awvon* here, it's clear in this text that the Israelites could suffer the consequences of both their ancestors' faults and their own personal faults. The notion of generational linkage is equally evident when authors use different words to distinguish between the sins of the fathers and those of the sons. For example, David uses four words in Psalm 32. According to Pastor Ken Fish[29], the word *peshaw* suggests voluntary rebellion that deviates from the purpose of divine law. *Chattah* is the usual term for "sin" or "offense"; it also includes unintentional faults. *Awvon* applies to sins with consequences. Here, David speaks of "imputing" iniquity, which limits the meaning, in this context, to attributing consequences to someone else. Finally, *remeeyaw* refers to an action like fraud or a passive attitude like negligence.

---

29 Live Conference On line, January 22-23, 2021. Anderson (Shannae), Hutchkin (Mike), Fish (Ken), Healing Generational Trauma Conference, videos 2 and 4. https://awakenedto.life/store/ministry-training/healing-trauma-and-ptsd/healing-generational-trauma-conference-january-2021-video-recordings/

> *Blessed is he whose transgression* (peshaw) *is forgiven,*
> *whose sin* (chattah) *is covered.*
> *Blessed is the man to whom the Lord imputes not iniquity* (awvon),
> *and in whose spirit there is no guile* (remeeyaw).
>
> Psalms 32:1-2

Also, the mage and prophet Daniel uses the word *khate*, derived from *chattah*, and the word *awvon* to distinguish the faults of his generation from those of their ancestors.

> *O Lord, according to all your righteousness,*
> *I beseech you, let your anger and your fury be turned away*
> *from your city Jerusalem, your holy mountain:*
> *because for our sins* (khate),
> *and for the iniquities of our fathers* (awvon),
> *Jerusalem and your people are become a reproach*
> *to all that are about us.*
>
> Daniel 9:16

The same terminology is used in a passage from the book of Nehemiah, this Jewish priest who returned from Babylon to lead the reconstruction of the wall of Jerusalem. One day, Nehemiah convenes a general assembly to read the Law and pray.

> *And the seed of Israel*
> *separated themselves from all strangers,*
> *and stood and confessed their sins* (khata),
> *and the iniquities* (awvon) *of their fathers.*
>
> Nehemiah 9:2

Here, these same two words are again used by Nehemiah to distinguish personal sins for which we are guilty from sins for which we inherit consequences through generational lines. However, it is worth noting that the context (Neh 9:24, 32, 36; 13:18) is linked to the notion of covenant, which we will discuss in the next chapter. For now, let's say that the Mosaic covenant stipulated that curses would result from the people's disobedience to this covenant. Nehemiah intercedes for a people who did not uphold the Old Covenant. His prayer targets the entire nation, whereas a prayer for generational links would be limited to a family line. However, the principle is the same: praying to cover the fault of ancestors and thus requesting the cancellation of consequences for descendants.

Why did these men of God bother to distinguish personal sins from iniquities ingrained in the generational line? First, because they were aware of the existence of such ancestral iniquities. Secondly, because they understood that these sins are not treated by God in the same way as our own faults. They affect us even if we are not guilty of them.

And this is still true today for those who live under the New Covenant. For example, Pastor Ken Fish, who has a ministry of healing and deliverance, gave a teaching on iniquities in which he recounted an experience that clearly demonstrates the reality of generational links[30]. A man who professed the Christian faith was blind as a result of nuclear medicine treatment aimed at eliminating a melanoma from his retina. Upon questioning him, Pastor Fish noted that this man's grandfather was a dowser[31]. He then asked this blind man to implore God's forgiveness for the sin of his ancestor, and he was healed of his blindness. This striking illustration demonstrates that the iniquity of his grandfather – in this case, an occult practice – had consequences for him, even though he was a Christian.

Science and intergenerationnal

We can connect some scientific discoveries with the theological concepts we have just discussed. Over the last decade, researcher

---

30 Fish (Ken), *Iniquities,* CD-rom. His teaching on CD doesn't seem to be available for sale on Ken Fish's website anymore.
31 A dowser searches for water, typically using rods, in order to dig wells. Many Christians consider this technique to be part of occult activities (divination) forbidden by the Lord.

Brian Dias from the School of Medicine at Emory University in Atlanta observed that mice simultaneously exposed to a smell of acetophenone (similar to that of Cherry Blossom) and electric shocks could transmit to their babies an increased sensitivity to this smell and fear of it, even in the absence of electric shocks. Dias observed in the next generation of mice an increase in the number of M-71 olfactory receptors, as well as the size of the brain area responsible for perceiving this particular smell. Brian Dias and Kerry Ressler were then able to reproduce this by inseminating mice with the sperm of electrified mice to eliminate the possibility that transmission was the result of parental education. They observed that the transmission of fear and sensitivity to the smell persisted up to the "third" generation[32].

This kind of research has multiplied since the 2000s, sparking keen interest in the scientific community to the point of transforming our understanding of genetics and creating a new sub-discipline: epigenetics. The concept is as follows: although the genetic code itself is not modifiable, the methylation and demethylation of certain DNA nucleotides (addition or removal of a carbon atom and three hydrogen atoms, CH3) would alter gene function. Indeed, DNA is an immense chain of smaller molecules called "nucleotides." One of these nucleic bases is cytosine. It seems that strong methylation of cytosines on DNA leads to low gene expression, while demethylation, on the contrary, usually activates them from their hibernation[33]. A similar phenomenon also occurs at the level of histones: proteins that serve to condense or decondense nuclear DNA, thereby modulating gene

---

32 Geddes (Linda), « Fear of a smell can be passed down several generations », Decembre First, 2013, [On line] https://www.newscientist.com/article/dn24677-fear-of-a-smell-can-be-passed-down-several-generations/#ixzz6xcUqwcag (June 12, 2021).
   (Tanya), « Fearful Experiences Passed On In Mouse Families », Decembre 5, 2013, [On line] https://www.livescience.com/41717-mice-inherit-fear-scents-genes.html (June 12, 2021).
33 « Épigénétique », Futura Santé, [En ligne] https://www.futura-sciences.com/sante/definitions/genetique-epigenetique-136/ (May 5, 2021).

replication. Epigenetics is thus the study of the control centers of gene expression. The role of these strategic locations would be to enable the species to adapt to certain environmental stressors.

> […] In response to the stress detected by the cell, a cascade of events will first lead to the removal of the methyl group located at a specific position of a gene encoding for a defense protein; by removing this methyl, the expression of this gene is no longer repressed, and the defense protein can therefore be produced to protect the cell[34].

Researchers are now attempting to produce drugs capable of modifying our genes to combat cancer. But epigenetics could also explain many behaviors, and even lead to trials aimed at modifying them. Scientists are now asking several questions. Faced with a powerful and constant stimulus, can the change persist for several generations? Could there be permanent changes?

We could add the following questions to this list: If the fear of electric shocks can be transmitted to the offspring of mice, is it possible for humans to pass on their fears to their descendants? If such mice are afraid even in the absence of shocks, could humans be afraid without reason due to ancestral traumas? Could these fears be maladaptive? For example, it was normal for my grandfather to be afraid during the war, but if children and grandchildren inherit the same fear and similar behaviors once the war is over, how can that be useful? Is epigenetics one of the mechanisms by which God acts to perpetuate curses for four or five generations? Can sins and traumas trigger nucleotide demethylation and modifications on histone? Could prayer modify these biochemical phenomena?

---

34 Trescases (Nathalie), Thorin (Eric), « L'épigénétique ? Jamais entendu parler… », April 11, 2017, [On line] https://observatoireprevention.org/2017/04/11/epigenetique-jamais-entenu-parler/ (May 5, 2021).

Another experiment reported by the pastor and prophet John Sanford might also explain the observed variability in the tendency to sin.

If we train a rat to respond to a light by rewarding it with food, it will eventually learn to salivate at the appearance of the light. After approximately seventeen generetaions, rats will be born already knowing to respond to light for food[35].

In the experiment I mentioned earlier, fear was inherited by mice as early as the next generation, while it took repeating a stimulus for many generations to modify the behavior of rats. However, this concerns the complete loss of a vital function that could lead to their death, as these rats will seek light, thinking they can be fed. This change is therefore much more radical than the transmission of fear.

What interests us here is the extrapolation of this model to humans. Could repeated traumas over several generations drastically influence the behavior of certain ethnicities? We can also wonder if the perversion of our carnal appetites does not stem from a genetics corrupted by the stimulation of wrongful desires for generations. And if human corruption could be evolutionary, sins practiced from generation to generation could lead to epigenetic changes that cause an increasing tendency to sin in descendants. Socially, this could explain why a nation may gradually sink into certain sins. We indeed see this progression at the beginning of the book of Genesis. Fortunately, we also observe the opposite: a nation can turn to God and return to more just principles[36].

---

35 Sandford (John & Paula), *The Elijah Task*, Tulsa [OK], Victory House, 1977, p. 127.

36 The Holy Spirit transforms the behavior of believers. Could the mass conversion of a nation also have epigenetic consequences that would reduce our tendency to commit evil?

According to researchers, one thing is certain: it seems that our understanding of genetics will never be the same. For example, Marcus Pembrey from the University of Bristol commented:

> It is high time public-health researchers took human transgenerational responses seriously. [...] I suspect we will not understand the rise in neuropsychiatric disorders or obesity, diabetes and metabolic disruptions generally, without taking a multigenerational approach[37].

Individualism that blinds us

I believe that the intergenerational transmission of sins and curses was better understood in the cultural contexts of the biblical characters' lives. Indeed, today, we conceive notions of justice on a very individualistic basis. For this reason, the word "iniquity" tends to be used as a synonym for personal sin in the French language, or not used at all. The idea that the sins of our ancestors can affect us is also largely forgotten in the body of Christ.

Lifestyle was more communal in the past. The Israelite nation was divided into tribes, like most peoples around them. The tribal mentality was that of a large family. There was solidarity. People fought together to survive, and they protected the honor of the group. This tribal organization also conveyed the idea of intervening on entire clans, rather than limiting punishment to only the guilty individuals. The story of Achan is instructive in this regard. At that time, the people of Israel began to invade the land of Canaan under the leadership of Joshua. God had ordered everything to be destroyed and to keep no spoils for oneself. However, Achan decided to keep a beautiful cloak, silver, and gold, which he hid in his tent (Jos 7:1). This resulted in the loss of the battle fought against the tiny village of Ai. The Israelites were

---

37 Geddes (Linda), *op. cit.* See note 32.

humiliated and confused. Joshua prostrated himself before God and implored Him. The Lord told him that everything was simply explained by the transgression of divine order. He revealed to him what had happened and what had affected their collective destiny:

> *Israel has sinned,*
> *and they have also transgressed my covenant*
> *which I commanded them:*
> *for they have even taken of the accursed thing,*
> *and have also stolen, and dissembled also,*
> *and they have put it even among their own stuff.*
> Joshua 7:11

Note that God does not immediately say, "Achan has sinned." Sin, dishonor, and failure fell upon everyone. But that did not prevent a specific judgment from being pronounced. So, God said to Joshua:

> *In the morning therefore you shall be brought*
> *according to your tribes:*
> *and it shall be, that the tribe which the LORD takes*
> *shall come according to the families thereof;*
> *and the family which the LORD shall take*
> *shall come by households;*
> *and the household which the LORD shall take*
> *shall come man by man.*
> Joshua 7:14

The text does not specify how the guilty party was discerned. Probably by using the Urim and Thummim from the breastplate of judgment worn by the high priest. The tribe of Judah was identified, then the family of Zerah (Achan's great-grandfather), and the household of Zabdi (the grandfather). Finally, Achan, the grandson of Zabdi, was found guilty. Once discovered, he publicly confessed his wrongdoing, and the items were found in his tent as evidence of his guilt. He, along with his sons and daughters, was then seized, and his entire family was stoned (Jos 7:24-25).

We may wonder here whether the people had followed the Law correctly by stoning Achan's children because according to the Law, each person was to pay for their own wrongdoing. I am inclined to believe that Joshua was a good judge, as he had been meticulously trained by Moses. Undoubtedly, he must have established that Achan's children were complicit with their father. If they had not conspired in the theft with him, they must have at least known that these items were hidden in their tent because it is difficult to conceal so much valuable property in a tent and go unnoticed! Therefore, I think that, in this specific case, Achan's children were punished because they had participated in their father's crime[38].

This story demonstrates the mentality and operation of a tribal society in which the behavior of some influences that of others. This communal mindset in social life also existed outside the people of Israel. For example, we see jealous individuals plotting to accuse Daniel to adore only Yahweh, after he was appointed one of the three chief governors of the Medo-Persian Empire. Found guilty, he is thrown into the lions' den. However, they do not harm or eat him. Witnessing the miracle, King Darius orders that all those who accused Daniel be thrown to the lions with their wives and children (Dan 6:24). Here, I doubt that the children of the leaders who conspired against Daniel participated in the plot. However, Darius did not act according to the same law as in Israel. While the communal aspect was similar for the Jews as in the Ancient World, there was still a major distinction: their law

---

[38] Another argument to support this position is that God did not punish the children of Korah during a similar rebellion (Num 16:27-33). Only the followers of Korah, Dathan, and Abiram died. Their children survived (Num 26:9-11). To support this, some Bible translates the Hebrew word "adam" in Numbers 16:32 as "followers." Another way to interpret these two passages would be to understand that the children of these three families were swallowed up by the earth (the word "adam" can also refer to the ground, the earth), but they survived unlike their parents. However, this interpretation seems less likely to me.

stipulated that only the guilty should be punished. This is also evident in another episode, this time from the life of Joash:

> *[...] he slew his servants which had slain the king his father.*
> *But the children of the murderers he slew not:*
> *according to that which is written in the book of the law of Moses,*
> *wherein the LORD commanded, saying,*
> *The fathers shall not be put to death for the children,*
> *nor the children be put to death for the fathers;*
> *but every man shall be put to death for his own sin.*
>
> 2 Kings 14:5-6

The concept of individual justice was taught in Israel, but the notions of interdependence, collective honor, and shared curses resulting from the sins of the fathers were also part of that culture and biblical teachings. The justice exercised toward each individual did not exclude the sharing of a collective destiny. They experienced the consequences of actions committed by others on each other. Thus, they were much less resistant than we are to the idea that the sins of ancestors could affect future generations. This is also why they prayed with a communal vision to be delivered from the consequences of sins committed by previous generations. They asked for forgiveness for the sins of their fathers, not to erase their guilt, but to avert the consequences from their descendants, imploring the mercy of the Lord.

> *O remember not against us former iniquities* (awvon)*:*
> *let your tender mercies speedily prevent us:*
> *for we are brought very low.*
> *Help us, O God of our salvation, for the glory of your name:*
> *and deliver us, and purge away our sins* (khataw)*,*
> *for your name's sake.*
>
> Psalms 79:8-9

In short, the entire Bible teaches the same thing. Children inherit the tendency to repeat sins, as well as the curses that result from the sins of their ancestors. However, concerning guilt and condemnation, each will be judged on an individual basis. We can only be judged and condemned if we ourselves commit sins. We inherit the burden of our ancestors' mistakes but not the guilt of their sins.

> *Our fathers have sinned, and are not;*
> *and we have borne their iniquities.*
>
> Lamentations 5:7

3
Alliances

As we have previously emphasized, the alliances made between God and humans also determine the destiny of humanity. The breaking of an alliance has consequences. For example, the alliance with Adam was broken, resulting in original curses. Therefore, Adam's sin is not merely an isolated moral act. It is a violation of a pre-established agreement between human beings and their Creator.

Human alliances

When made among humans, an alliance is a permanent legal arrangement, a sacred promise based on mutual trust that involves the reputation of both parties. An alliance is more than a contract. The latter is rather based on distrust – aiming to ensure one receives their due – and is only made for a specified duration, while an alliance is permanent and honor-bound. It is a commitment for life, favorable to one another, no matter what happens.

Just like the breaking of a divine alliance, disregarding a human alliance can affect future generations. For instance, marriage is a human alliance that God instituted when He presented Eve to Adam. All humans are obligated to honor this divine institution. The prophet Malachi states that disrespecting this alliance results in losing God's favor, wherein He disregards offerings and prayers (Mal 2:13-16). This text speaks of consequences for the entire people when a society veers away from honoring marriage. Jesus also speaks against divorce, recalling the Creator's original intention (Mt 19:3-8). He says that marriage was established to be permanent, with one man united to one woman.

The following story is another example of curses resulting from the disrespect of a human alliance. Gibeon was one of the cities targeted by Joshua's invasion of Canaan. However, to avoid being annihilated, the citizens of this city resorted to trickery. They pretended to be a people from a distant land and offered to be servants to Israel forever in exchange for their protection. The Israelites did not consult God and were deceived. Once this alliance was made, the Israelite people had to respect the oath they made before God (Josh 9:14-20). However, two centuries later, King Saul decided to eliminate these Gibeonites who still lived among them. Several years passed, and a great famine struck Israel for three years. King David was in power at the time. He prayed, and God revealed to him that the cause of this calamity was the breaking of the distant alliance with the Gibeonites. David then negotiated with the surviving representatives of the Gibeonites who had been massacred by Saul. They reached an agreement: seven descendants of King Saul had to be killed to atone for the injustice committed by the Israelites. The famine ceased after their execution (2 Sam 21:1-6,14). We see here the significance of a disregarded alliance. When alliances are respected, there are no dire consequences. But when they are violated, as Saul did, it can have repercussions for an entire people. Indeed, it was only the generation following Saul's that suffered the famine, and it was Saul's descendants who were put to death to restore the situation. Disregarded alliances can thus lead to consequences for the descendants of the guilty, just as the sins of ancestors have consequences for future generations. God detests dishonoring His commitments, even if they are purely human alliances. The same holds true today. For example, we can compare these alliances to more recent agreements made between indigenous peoples and colonizing nations.

Other human alliances only apply to a family or a group of individuals. For instance, Abram made an alliance with Mamre when he settled in Canaan (Gen 14:13). Later, he made another alliance with King Abimelech (Gen 21:27,32). Such alliances included rules regarding the sharing of territory, possessions, and water sources, similar to those that still exist between multinational corporations and the countries where they exploit natural resources.

David and Jonathan also entered into a private alliance for mutual protection, which obligated the survivor to take care of the other's descendants (1 Sam 18:3; 20:12-16). Moreover, David showed kindness to Mephibosheth in memory of his father Jonathan (2 Sam 9). In this agreement, Jonathan also acknowledged the prophetic word of Samuel stating that David would be the future king. He thus relinquished the throne to which he was entitled as Saul's son (1 Sam 23:16-18).

A satanic agreement

We may question the nature of the exchanges between the early humans and Satan. Did they not enter into an agreement with God's adversary by accepting his words and eating from the forbidden tree? However, certain elements are missing here to speak of a true alliance. There was no new commitment made based on honor and mutual trust. Satan was not offering anything new to Eve. In fact, he was using what God had already declared: that Adam and Eve would be like gods. He added two new ideas: it was intriguing to know evil, and God did not want them to become gods. It is this same pride that had corrupted Satan and which is, even today, at the core of Satanism. In this case, it can be said to be more of a rebellious agreement aimed at thwarting a divine alliance. But if Adam and Eve did not enter into a true alliance with Satan, it is not an exaggeration to say that they followed his thinking and that this binds humanity today.

The early humans wanted to be more powerful and free when they accepted the words of God's enemy. But humans always lose when they compromise with the devil. Satan cannot create anything. He can only steal goods and redistribute them. When the original sin was consummated, the true winner was the devil. He thus stole authority from the only creature that had the mandate to rule the world and the power to resist evil on earth. His cunning allowed him to enslave humankind and become the prince of this world (Jn 12:31; 14:30; 16:11). The apostle Paul describes the condition of all humans before their conversion to Christianity in this way:

> *And you has he quickened,*
> *who were dead in trespasses and sins;*
> *Wherein in time past you walked*
> *according to the course of this world,*
> *according to the prince of the power of the air,*
> *the spirit that now works in the children of disobedience:*
> *Among whom also we all had our conversation*
> *in times past in the lusts of our flesh,*
> *fulfilling the desires of the flesh and of the mind;*
> *and were by nature the children of wrath, even as others.*
>
> Ephesians 2:1-3

Humans are now slaves to sin and collaborate with Satan, "the prince of the power of the air." They do not realize that this usurper has blinded their understanding (2 Cor 4:3-4). Too often, unbelievers do not understand their condition or the way out. In the latter passage, the Greek word translated as "understanding" is *noema*. It refers to the comprehension of things. Humans technically have the intelligence to deduce that God exists by observing creation, but this intelligence is "plunged into darkness" because they adopt another concept of governance and the origin of the world (Rom 1:20-21). They no longer have "eyes to see or ears to hear," as the prophets and apostles have said (Deut 29:4; Ezk 12:2; Mt 13:14-15; Rom 11:8).

Similarly, the problem is not that the human mind is dead, in the sense of being inactive. It is capable of spiritual activities like magic and religions that worship false gods (Gal 5:20). The true diagnosis is that it is incapable of turning to the only true God by its own strength. This true God (Father, Son, Spirit) must therefore intervene to free them from the bondage of sin and Satan who blinds them. He must deliver them from the power of darkness to translate them into the kingdom of His dear Son (Col 1:13). It is clear here that a first allegiance must be broken to create a new one. Jesus told his Jewish countrymen that their father was the devil (Jn 8:44) and that they would be slaves to sin until they believed in Him so that He could set them free (Jn 8:34,36).

Jesus highlighted the existence of two kingdoms: the kingdom of God and the kingdom of darkness. He affirms that whoever is not with Him is against Him (Lk 11:23). Peter Horrobin, founder of the international deliverance ministry Ellel Ministries, paraphrases this last passage and summarizes its context in three points: Satan's domination over the world, Christ's work to deliver us from it, and Church authority to continue to cast out demons and practice deliverance from every oppressive bond. He suggests an amplified and contextualized version of Lk 11:23 as follows:

> Anyone who is not for Me in the ministry of deliverance that God My Father has called Me into, as part of the full Gospel of evangelism, healing and deliverance, is really against Me for they are, either directly or indirectly, opposing a vital part of My work, which is given to Me by the Holy Spirit and which proves that the Kingdom of God has come[39].

There is no neutral zone. Jesus is the only way (Jn 14:6). No other religion leads to God the Father. It is not possible to go to heaven without believing in Jesus Christ because only He can deliver us from the grip of the devil on our lives. Only the New Covenant can set us free.

---

39 Horrobin (Peter J.), *Healing through Delivrance*, Grand Rapids [MI], Chosen, 2008, p. 224.

Divine covenants

Divine alliances are always initiated by God. They can be conditional or unconditional. They seek to define His relationship with humans. They teach what is right and wrong. The first covenant established by God was with Adam. The terms were that man should take care of everything on earth and could enjoy paradise. Only the tree of good and evil was forbidden. Adam also had access to God. He maintained a personal relationship with Him. All of this was lost, as humans preferred to rebel and follow the path of Satan. Curses have indeed resulted from this original sin.

Like the covenant with Adam, the Sinai covenant is another covenant containing conditions. The Law given to Israel through Moses specified what was right and wrong in order to enlighten the misguided human intelligence (Rom 3:20). It provided a code for judgment and punishment, reflecting the unchanging nature of God.

Moses' law thus promised a series of blessings for those who fulfilled it (Deut 28:1-14), while numerous curses threatened those who did not uphold this conditional covenant (Deut 28:15-68):

> *But it shall come to pass, if you will not listen*
> *to the voice of the LORD your God,*
> *to observe to do all his commandments and his statutes*
> *which I command you this day;*
> *that all these curses shall come on you, and overtake you:*
> *Cursed shall you be in the city,*
> *and cursed shall you be in the field.*
> *Cursed shall be your basket and your store.*
> *Cursed shall be the fruit of your body, and the fruit of your land,*
> *the increase of your cows, and the flocks of your sheep.*
> *Cursed shall you be when you come in,*
> *and cursed shall you be when you go out.*
> *The LORD shall send on you cursing, vexation, and rebuke,*

*in all that you set your hand to for to do,
until you be destroyed, and until you perish quickly;
because of the wickedness of your doings,
whereby you have forsaken me.
The LORD shall make the pestilence stick to you,
until he have consumed you from off the land,
where you go to possess it.
The LORD shall smite you with a consumption,
and with a fever, and with an inflammation,
and with an extreme burning, and with the sword,
and with blasting, and with mildew;
and they shall pursue you until you perish.
And your heaven that is over your head shall be brass,
and the earth that is under you shall be iron.
The LORD shall make the rain of your land powder and dust:
from heaven shall it come down on you, until you be destroyed.
The LORD shall cause you to be smitten before your enemies:
you shall go out one way against them,
and flee seven ways before them:
and shall be removed into all the kingdoms of the earth.
And your carcass shall be meat to all fowls of the air,
and to the beasts of the earth, and no man shall fray them away.
The LORD will smite you with the botch of Egypt,
and with the tumors, and with the scab, and with the itch,
whereof you can not be healed.
The LORD shall smite you with madness,
and blindness, and astonishment of heart:
And you shall grope at noonday, as the blind gropes in darkness,
and you shall not prosper in your ways:
and you shall be only oppressed and spoiled ever more,
and no man shall save you.
You shall betroth a wife, and another man shall lie with her:
you shall build an house, and you shall not dwell therein:
you shall plant a vineyard,
and shall not gather the grapes thereof.
Your ox shall be slain before your eyes,*

and you shall not eat thereof:
your ass shall be violently taken away from before your face,
and shall not be restored to you:
your sheep shall be given to your enemies,
and you shall have none to rescue them.
Your sons and your daughters shall be given to another people,
and your eyes shall look,
and fail with longing for them all the day long;
and there shall be no might in your hand.
The fruit of your land, and all your labors,
shall a nation which you know not eat up;
and you shall be only oppressed and crushed always:
So that you shall be mad for the sight
of your eyes which you shall see.
The LORD shall smite you in the knees, and in the legs,
with a sore botch that cannot be healed,
from the sole of your foot to the top of your head.
The LORD shall bring you,
and your king which you shall set over you,
to a nation which neither you nor your fathers have known;
and there shall you serve other gods, wood and stone.
And you shall become an astonishment, a proverb, and a byword,
among all nations where the LORD shall lead you.
You shall carry much seed out into the field,
and shall gather but little in; for the locust shall consume it.
You shall plant vineyards, and dress them,
but shall neither drink of the wine, nor gather the grapes;
for the worms shall eat them.
You shall have olive trees throughout all your coasts,
but you shall not anoint yourself with the oil;
for your olive shall cast his fruit.
You shall beget sons and daughters, but you shall not enjoy them;
for they shall go into captivity.
All your trees and fruit of your land shall the locust consume.
The stranger that is within you shall get up above you very high;
and you shall come down very low.

*He shall lend to you, and you shall not lend to him:
he shall be the head, and you shall be the tail.
Moreover, all these curses shall come on you,
and shall pursue you, and overtake you, till you be destroyed;
because you listened not to the voice of the LORD your God,
to keep his commandments and his statutes
which he commanded you:
And they shall be on you for a sign and for a wonder,
and on your seed for ever.
Because you served not the LORD your God with joyfulness,
and with gladness of heart, for the abundance of all things;
Therefore shall you serve your enemies
which the LORD shall send against you,
in hunger, and in thirst, and in nakedness,
and in want of all things:
and he shall put a yoke of iron on your neck,
until he have destroyed you.
The LORD shall bring a nation against you from far,
from the end of the earth, as swift as the eagle flies;
a nation whose tongue you shall not understand;
A nation of fierce countenance,
which shall not regard the person of the old,
nor show favor to the young:
And he shall eat the fruit of your cattle,
and the fruit of your land, until you be destroyed:
which also shall not leave you either corn, wine, or oil,
or the increase of your cows, or flocks of your sheep,
until he have destroyed you.
And he shall besiege you in all your gates,
until your high and fenced walls come down,
wherein you trusted, throughout all your land:
and he shall besiege you in all your gates
throughout all your land,
which the LORD your God has given you.
And you shall eat the fruit of your own body,
the flesh of your sons and of your daughters,*

*which the LORD your God has given you,
in the siege, and in the narrow place,
with which your enemies shall distress you:
So that the man that is tender among you, and very delicate,
his eye shall be evil toward his brother,
and toward the wife of his bosom,
and toward the remnant of his children which he shall leave:
So that he will not give to any of them
of the flesh of his children whom he shall eat:
because he has nothing left him in the siege,
and in the narrow place,
with which your enemies shall distress you in all your gates.
The tender and delicate woman among you,
which would not adventure to set the sole of her foot
on the ground for delicateness and tenderness,
her eye shall be evil toward the husband of her bosom,
and toward her son, and toward her daughter,
And toward her young one that comes out from between her feet,
and toward her children which she shall bear:
for she shall eat them for want of all things secretly
in the siege and narrow place,
with which your enemy shall distress you in your gates.
If you will not observe to do all the words of this law
that are written in this book,
that you may fear this glorious and fearful name,
THE LORD THY GOD;
Then the LORD will make your plagues wonderful,
and the plagues of your seed, even great plagues,
and of long continuance, and sore sicknesses,
and of long continuance.
Moreover, he will bring on you all the diseases of Egypt,
which you were afraid of; and they shall stick to you.
Also every sickness, and every plague,
which is not written in the book of this law,
them will the LORD bring on you, until you be destroyed.
And you shall be left few in number,*

whereas you were as the stars of heaven for multitude;
because you would not obey the voice of the LORD your God.
And it shall come to pass,
that as the LORD rejoiced over you to do you good,
and to multiply you;
so the LORD will rejoice over you to destroy you,
and to bring you to nothing;
and you shall be plucked from off the land
where you go to possess it.
And the LORD shall scatter you among all people,
from the one end of the earth even to the other;
and there you shall serve other gods,
which neither you nor your fathers have known,
even wood and stone.
And among these nations shall you find no ease,
neither shall the sole of your foot have rest:
but the LORD shall give you there a trembling heart,
and failing of eyes, and sorrow of mind:
And your life shall hang in doubt before you;
and you shall fear day and night,
and shall have none assurance of your life:
In the morning you shall say,
Would God it were even! and at even you shall say,
Would God it were morning!
for the fear of your heart with which you shall fear,
and for the sight of your eyes which you shall see.
And the LORD shall bring you into Egypt again with ships,
by the way whereof I spoke to you,
You shall see it no more again:
and there you shall be sold to your enemies for slaves
and bondwomen, and no man shall buy you.
Deuteronomy 28:15-68

Phew! What calamities! That sends a shiver down the spine. Despite His goodness, God allows evil to reach those who disobey. Being sovereign, He even takes responsibility for such curses, which quickly make us forget the blessings that precede them. But note that these calamities are not really new. They echo the consequences of original sin by describing difficulties related to family and work. They depict human wickedness and the degradation of creation. All these consequences of original sin are portrayed in more detail in Deuteronomy 28, but they are not a new addition to the human condition.

The law of Moses defined more clearly what is right and wrong. It also brought some hope by describing how to avoid sin and curse. There is in the Sinai law a theoretical possibility of bringing blessing to all who perfectly observe it. The problem is that no one was capable of this, because all humans have lost the power to do good and reflect the glory of God (Romans 3:23). The Jews could only rely on expiatory sacrifices for their sins when the Law was not observed. They could also appeal to the grace of God who had told them, even under the dispensation of the Law: "This commandment that I command you today is not too hard for you, neither is it far off.[40]" Nevertheless, the law is the law! This is what the apostle Paul reminds the Jews of his time. Salvation cannot come from obedience accomplished by their own strength. They should never have adopted such a legalistic attitude.

For as many as are of the works of the law
are under the curse: for it is written,
Cursed is every one that continues not in all things
which are written in the book of the law to do them.

Galatians 3:10

The history of the Israelites demonstrates these principles. Despite a glimmer of hope, the covenant of the Law ends in curses, just like the first Adamic covenant. However, it is worth noting that the consequences described in the Law do not refer, this time, to the original sin of Adam and Eve. Here, it is

---

40 Deuteronomy 30:11.

stipulated that it is disobedience to the covenant that will lead to the downfall of Israel. And, interestingly for our study, in reading Deuteronomy 28, we see that it is often the descendants who suffer the consequences of the ancestors' sins. This clearly shows that the curses continued to spread, not only through the phenomenon of generational ties stemming from the sins of the ancestors, but also through their disregard of the covenants. These calamities affected the children of the Jews who did not respect God's Law, and unfortunately, this was inevitable due to human weakness.

The transmission of hope

Since His people were unable to uphold conditional covenants, could God establish a covenant without conditions? Of course! The Bible describes several unconditional covenants through which God offers His help purely by grace. Thus, He makes a covenant with Noah at the beginning of human history. The Creator looks upon the earth and sees that all flesh is corrupt. It is full of violence. So God tells Noah that He intends to destroy everything but to spare his life, and that of his family, to repopulate the world (Gen 6:11-14). He sends the rain, and after the flood, God says:

> *And I will establish my covenant with you,*
> *neither shall all flesh be cut off any more*
> *by the waters of a flood;*
> *neither shall there any more be a flood to destroy the earth.*
> *And God said,*
> *This is the token of the covenant*
> *which I make between me and you*
> *and every living creature*
> *that is with you, for perpetual generations:*
> *I do set my bow in the cloud,*
> *and it shall be for a token of a covenant*
> *between me and the earth.*
>
> Genesis 9:11-13

This episode in history teaches us that God detests sin and can judge the world in a terrible way. But He can also show grace to whomever He chooses. However, the Noahic covenant did not solve the problem of our fallen nature. Noah's descendants gradually fell back into the same sins as their ancestors. That's why God chose Abram. He invited him to leave his country, to trust Him (Heb 11:8), and to follow Him. He promised him a new land (Gen 15:18) and told him that his descendants would be multiplied there. This man would become the father of a multitude of nations (Gen 17:2,4). His name, Abram [high father], would be changed to Abraham [father of a multitude] (Gen 17:5). Abram's call marked the choice of a people, both in terms of race and election through faith. Indeed, Abraham is the father of Israel, just as he is the father of the Church (Gal 3:7-9). But once again, the Abrahamic covenant did not stop original sin and the curses that follow from generation to generation. It only paved the way for the New Covenant.

The covenant between God and David is also an unconditional, unilateral, and eternal grace (2 Sam 23:5) by which God promises David to build him a temple himself. He pledges to establish his throne forever (2 Sam 7:11-16). His son Solomon built the temple that David had envisioned. However, David's descendants ceased to reign during the deportation of the people to Babylon. The curses mentioned in the Mosaic law were fulfilled because of idolatry and violence. How is this possible since the covenant with David was unconditional? The authors of the New Testament enlighten us on this point by indicating the dual meaning of the promise made to David. Indeed, it could only find its full realization in Jesus Christ, this descendant of David whose body was the temple of God (Jn 2:19-21), and who now reigns at the right hand of God (Mt 26:64; Heb 8:1; 12:2).

Thus, it was towards the New Covenant that all conditional and unconditional covenants pointed and converged. They informed us about what was to come. Jesus is the new sinless Adam who gives life (Rom 5:19; 1 Cor 15:45). There will be no other flood, but there will be judgment, and, like in the time of Noah, those who believe in Jesus will be taken away before that terrible day; this time, not in an ark, but on the clouds, to be with the Lord (Mt 24:37-39; 1 Thess 4:17). The disciples of the Messiah are believers like Abraham. Finally, the prophecies made to David are fulfilled by the coming of the Lord Jesus, who is the king of kings (1 Tim 6:14-15).

As for the Mosaic covenant, God had announced to Moses the coming of a prophet like him, to whom they should obey (Deut 18:15; Acts 3:22; 7:37). Moreover, the sacrifices of the Mosaic law could only temporarily cover sins. The day would come when Jesus' sacrifice would take away the sin of the world (Isa 53:4-12; Jn 1:29).

By so much was Jesus made a surety of a better testament.
[...] For such an high priest became us,
who is holy, harmless, undefiled, separate from sinners,
and made higher than the heavens;
Who needs not daily, as those high priests,
to offer up sacrifice, first for his own sins,
and then for the people's:
for this he did once, when he offered up himself.

Hebrew 7.22,26-27

Each time a new covenant was established, it revealed a new aspect of salvation to humanity. But all these covenants find their full significance in Christ. Thus, from the beginning, God had a plan to redeem humanity, and Jesus' death on the cross definitively cancelled the guilt stemming from disobedience to conditional covenants.

Blotting out the handwriting of ordinances that was against us,
which was contrary to us,
and took it out of the way, nailing it to his cross;

Colossians 2:14

It's as if God said, "Look, these unkept covenants can no longer condemn you now, for my Son has endured the punishment in your place. These legal acts can no longer accuse you!" All conditional covenants were legal acts that judged humans. But here's the Good News: at the cross, death can no longer have victory over the Church (Mt 16:18).

From one covenant to another, there is rupture, but also a common thread that integrates them into a predetermined plan. All these covenants and beautiful promises were entrusted to Israel (Rom 9:4). This people preserved and transmitted this heritage. They conveyed the hope of the Messiah. Note that this passing on of covenants was relayed from generation to generation, and one day, the Messiah himself came from this people. All of this is represented as a transferable seed that passes from Adam to Seth, then to Noah, then to Shem. It is given to Abraham, to Isaac, and to Jacob. It is passed on to David, to arrive at Joseph, the adoptive father of Jesus. That's why the Jews insist on genealogies. Even the New Testament is interested in them (Mt 1:1-17; Lk 3:23-38). The New Covenant, however, is not the result of racial belonging (Jn 1:13). Nevertheless, Christianity is grafted onto the Jewish heritage (Rom 11:17). That's why we speak of Judeo-Christianity. It is the result of a long intergenerational process. In his commentary on Rom 11:13-24, William Barclay says this about the transmission of covenants:

> What Paul deduces from that is this: the patriarchs were sacred to God; they had in a special way heard God's voice and obeyed God's Word; in a special way, they had been chosen and consecrated by God. From them the whole nation sprang; and just as the first consecrated handful of dough made the whole lump sacred and the dedication of the sapling made the whole tree sacred, so the consecration of its. There is truth here. The remnant in Israel did not make themselves what they were; they inherited faith from their ancestors before them. Every one of us lives to some extent on the spiritual capital of the past. None of us is self-made. We are what godly

parents and ancestors have made us; and, even if we strayed fare away and shamed our heritage, we cannot totally separate ourselves from the goodness and faithfulness that made us what we are[41].

Jesus came to free the Jews from the conditional covenants they could not keep. Through him, the unconditional promises made to the fathers of faith, such as Noah, Abraham, and David, are now accessible to all peoples (Rom 15:8-12). But what will happen to Israel, who received these promises and yet rejected Christ? God is faithful. He "does not repent of his gifts and his calling" (Rom 11:29). What he promises, he fulfills perfectly (Num 23:19). Hasn't God promised them an everlasting covenant (Gen 17:7-8; Gal 3:6-29) and victory over their enemies (Gen 22:17)? For this reason, Paul explains that the Jews were temporarily rejected because of their inability to recognize Jesus as their Messiah; but shortly before his return, "they will look on him whom they have pierced" (Zech 12:10; Jn 19:37; Rev 1:7), Jesus, and "thus all Israel will be saved" (Rom 11:26). Christ will then prove to the Jews "the truthfulness of God in confirming the promises made to the fathers" (Rom 15:8).

Covenants and generational ties

People who do not believe in generational inheritances insist on Christ's victory to say that we can no longer be affected by the curses resulting from the sins of our ancestors. As for me, I believe, in light of Scripture, that Christ's victory does not eliminate generational ties. However, it offers us the opportunity to pray in a new way, as we will see in the continuation of this book.

Divine alliances do not completely deliver us from evil in the present time. We have seen that the Noahic covenant did not make

---

41 Barclay (William), *The New Daily Study Bible – The letters to the Romans*, London, Westminster John Knox Press, 2002, p. 176.

sin disappear. Similarly, God's favor on Abraham did not make him perfect. Even the New Covenant, which promises us total deliverance from our human condition at the end of times, does not guarantee us complete victory over sin right now. Speaking of Jesus Christ, the Bible affirms this.

> *You have put all things in subjection under his feet.*
> *For in that he put all in subjection under him,*
> *he left nothing that is not put under him.*
> *But now we see not yet all things put under him.*
>
> Hebrews 2.8

Divine alliances offer a protective umbrella. Human condition would be worse outside of these alliances, but it is not perfect within them either. Take, for example, poverty. If you are born into a poor family, with few exceptions, you will suffer the consequences attached to it, even if you are a devout Jew and even if you become a Christian during your life. The same goes for all the curses attached to our sinful condition. We are still mortal and afflicted by illness. Is it not illogical, then, to believe that all generational ties will be erased as soon as a person converts? The New Covenant does not automatically eradicate all these curses, any more than the Old Covenant. It guarantees more complete promises, but not all deliverance occurs automatically upon conversion.

Another argument sometimes put forward by theologians opposed to the notion of generational ties is that the Law no longer applies to Christians. For them, the second commandment of the Law, often used to defend the existence of generational ties (Ex 20:5), would not apply in the New Covenant. Yet, Jesus said he did not come to abolish the Law (Mt 5:17). He came to fulfill it, meaning to die on the cross so that our sins could be forgiven and we could receive the Spirit of God, enabling us to obey the Law more easily. This is what the prophets had announced (Jer 31:33; Ezk 36:26). Paul also asserts that Christians experience this reality today (Rom 8:8-9; Gal 5:17). That's why Jews and Gentiles who convert to Christianity are all bound to obey the ethics of the Law by the power of the Spirit. Therefore, if animal sacrifices and rituals of the Law can cease because Jesus is the final complete sacrifice, we must not conclude that we can abolish the ethics of the Law (Mt 5:19). As Christians, we still rely on the Law to know what is right or wrong. And this new law of the Spirit within us (Rom 8:2-4) is, in fact, an impulse to pursue the deeper purpose of the Mosaic law, which is to love God and neighbor with all our hearts (Lk 10:25-28). The Ten Commandments are therefore still relevant today, as they summarize the Lord's ethics. Thus, the first precept orders not to have other gods besides the one and only true God, the Eternal, the Creator. The third commandment says not to use the name of God in vain (blasphemy, etc.). In the second commandment, which interests us here, God says He is jealous and does not tolerate the worship of the creature. He speaks against any form of representation of heavenly or earthly things (angels, creatures, etc.). And it is in this context that He declares: "I am a jealous God, punishing the iniquity of the fathers on the children to the third and fourth generations of those who hate me, and showing mercy to thousands of generations of those who love me and keep my commandments (Ex 20.5-6)." By what right would we eliminate this notion of generational transmission included in the second commandment?

God desires to bless those who respect His alliances. But in His justice, He also imposes the original curse on those who reject the coverage of the alliances through practices contrary to them, such as idolatry, occultism, witchcraft, and false religions. This judgment is not new. The person who associates with Satan is doomed to perdition. There is no salvation outside of God's alliances. That's why Jesus said that whoever does not believe in Him is already judged (Jn 3:18). It is still true today that idolatry and occultism have consequences for the descendants of all those who engage in these practices.

Furthermore, this text reveals that God's goodness surpasses His strictness in being just. The numbers here represent God's compassionate character. The number "thousand" denotes a very prolonged, indefinite, or eternal period. This shows that God does not forget His alliances. This number contrasts with the "three or four" generations that may suffer curses. But this latter number is also symbolic. This period can be shorter. For example, the Jewish people returned from their exile in Babylon in less than two generations. It can be longer. Indeed, the descendants of an illegitimate child were to be excommunicated according to the Law for up to the tenth generation (Deut 23:2). Therefore, we should look at the proportion of the numbers rather than their absolute value. The relative duration of generational blessings and curses highlights the gracious character of a God who desires to forgive repentant humans and bless their descendants (Ex 34:6; Ezk 18:23). But God is also just. He punishes the guilty. And children can inherit the consequences of their fathers' sins.

In summary, alliances establish rules governing relationships between humans or between God and humans. They teach what is right or wrong. They all converge toward the New Covenant. They shape the destiny of humans, but for now, they do not resolve the question of the presence of sin and evil in the world. Among other things, entering into an alliance does not automatically cancel out negative generational inheritances. These stem from both sin and the disregard of alliances. The second commandment clearly shows that idolatry and occult practices produce curses stemming from both condemnable sins and disobedience to a divine alliance. The theologian Charles Hodge, even though he believed in the doctrine of federalism that we reject, explains well the notion of generational ties stemming from the fall and the disregard of alliances.

> This representative principle pervades the whole Scriptures. The imputation of Adam's sin to his posterity is not an isolated fact. It is only an illustration of a general principle which characterizes the dispensations of God from the beginning

of the world. [...] Esau's selling his birhtrigt, shut out his descendants from the covenant of promise. The children of Moab and Ammon were excluded from the congregation of the Lord forever, because their ancestors opposed the Israelite when they came out of Egypt. [...] God said to Eli that the iniquity of his house should not be purged with sacrifice and offering forever. To David it was said, "The sword shall nerver depart from thy house; because thou hast despised me, and hast taken the wife of Uriah the Hittite to be thy wife." To the disobedient Gehazi it was said: "The leprosy of Naaman shall cleave unto thee and unto thy seed forever." The sin of Jeroboam and of the men of his generation determined the destiny of the ten tribes for all time. The imprecation of the Jews, when they demanded the crucifixion of Christ, "His blood be on us and on our children," still weighs down the scattered people of Israel. [...] This principle runs through the whole Scriptures. [...] Children suffered equally with adults in the judgments, whether famine, pestilence, or war, which came upon the people for their sins[42].

If we understand that humans are cursed because of original sin and that this has generational consequences; if we grasp that alliances do not eliminate evil from this world; if we assimilate the idea that sins are distributed differently from one family to another due to the inheritance of certain sins; if we accept that our ancestors, whether born again or not, may have been affected by the consequences of their ancestors' sins; then we must also admit that some of the sins of those who preceded us in our family lineage may affect us. And, we should then learn to pray to break our generational ties.

---

42 Hodge (Charles), *op.cit.*, pp. 198-199.

4
Annoyed teeth

After the reigns of David and Solomon, the Israelite people neglected their alliances. They turned to other gods. They ceased offering sacrifices to the Lord and forgot His ordinances. God sent prophets to bring them back to order and to deliver a message of hope: one day, a new covenant will come that will be different from all others, and the human condition will be restored.

The prophecies announcing the coming of the Messiah were scattered and incomplete. Like pieces of a puzzle, one had to study all the prophetic books to reconstruct it. Some apparent contradictions clouded the picture. Thus, there was mention of both a glorious Messiah coming to deliver the people and a suffering lamb enduring punishment in place of humans. How to reconcile the two? It was only with the coming of Jesus Christ and the announcement of His future return that we could understand that these prophecies would be fulfilled in two stages. In the first stage, the Messiah came to die for all the sins of humanity. Note, moreover, that the New Covenant in His blood would have effects not only on our personal sins (*pesha*) but also on the iniquities (*awvon*) committed by our ancestors.

> *But he was wounded for our transgressions (pesha),*
> *he was bruised for our iniquities (awvon):*
> *the chastisement of our peace was on him;*
> *and with his stripes we are healed.*
>
> Isaiah 53:5

An enigmatic metaphor

Among the pieces of the prophetic puzzle, there is a proverb that was cited in Israel. We find it in two places, in Ezekiel 18:2 and Jeremiah 31:29. These texts are regularly used to contradict the existence of generational ties. According to some, they indicate that in the New Covenant, we are no longer guilty of the sins of our ancestors, and we no longer suffer the consequences. However, if this understanding is correct, it implies that original sin no longer has an effect on Christians. But this understanding is mistaken.

Let's now study the context of these two chapters to better understand the message these prophets wished to convey. Let's start with Ezekiel 18. Several commentators say that there is no mention here of a new covenant as in Jeremiah. Nevertheless, Ezekiel speaks of the importance of having a new heart and spirit (v. 31-32). This new spirit opposes the idea that children must die for the sins of their fathers or that fathers must die for the sins of their children (vv. 19, 25). God desires to forgive the sins of those who repent (vv. 21-28). It is in this context that the proverb is cited:

> *What mean you, that you use this proverb*
> *concerning the land of Israel, saying,*
> *The fathers have eaten sour grapes,*
> *and the children's teeth are set on edge?*
> *As I live, said the Lord GOD,*
> *you shall not have occasion any more*
> *to use this proverb in Israel.*
> *Behold, all souls are mine;*
> *as the soul of the father, so also the soul of the son is mine:*
> *the soul that sins, it shall die.*
>
> Ezekiel 18:2-4

The prophet here recalls a principle already stated in the Law of Moses. Let's remember that Deuteronomy 24:16 stated it very clearly: "Fathers shall not be put to death because of their children, nor shall children be put to death because of their fathers; each one shall be put to death for his own sin[43]." God has always said that we do not inherit the guilt of our ancestors, but only the consequences of their sins.

However, Israel was exposed to the customs of foreign nations that punished the entire family of those found guilty with death[44]. The maxim of the sour grapes illustrates these legal rules imported from pagan nations: children are affected by the bad fruits consumed by their fathers. Many Israelites in exile had come to believe that children must pay with their lives for the sins of their fathers (v. 19) or that fathers must pay for the sins of their children (vv. 5, 11, 13). Some theologians even think that the children of Israel had come to interpret the second commandment (Ex 20:3-6; Deut 5:9-10) in this way because of pagan influence. The curses poured out on three or four generations would have been the result of guilt received from ancestors, which aligns with the principle of federalism. These children who had inherited the guilt of their fathers logically had to suffer penalties just like them.

Yet, God had always opposed this. It was necessary to have a good knowledge of the Law to understand that one could inherit the consequences of the sins of ancestors without being guilty, and therefore without having to be condemned by a human court. But it was easy for them to forget this nuance after the chosen people had undergone deportation. Many had died during this exile. They now lived in slavery. They must have felt guilty following this divine judgment. However, if we rely on the Law, God judged guilty before His throne only those who had sinned.

---

43 See discussion on this passage in chapter 2.
44 See discussion on Daniel 6:24 at the end of chapter 2. Ezekiel lived in exile in Babylon, just like Daniel. Their ministries intersected. They both interacted with a Jewish community partially assimilated by the surrounding Babylonian culture.

Certainly, these Jews collectively bore the burden of a certain guilt associated with the past. That is why God specifies to them, through the mouth of the prophet Ezekiel, that the guilt of their ancestors is not passed on to them. Ezekiel thus corrects this erroneous pagan way of thinking and reminds them that each one must be condemned for his own sin (vv. 3, 20).

Ezekiel 18 would therefore have nothing to do with the announcement of the New Covenant. The future tense used in verse 3 to say "you shall no longer repeat this proverb" simply indicates that these practices will cease once the corrective teaching of the prophet has been grasped by the Jewish community. Thus, Ezekiel 18 is just an exhortation from God. The prophet first describes the fatalistic and erroneous attitude adopted by the people. Then, he reminds of the distinction made by the Law of Moses between fault (guilt) and consequences. He does not announce any change to this Law. The consequences (curses) for the children will continue if the sins of the fathers do not cease. But the children will not be guilty for them.

Announcing a New Covenant

The context of Jeremiah 31 is different. This prophet lived a little before Ezekiel, although their ministries overlapped. However, Jeremiah did not live in Babylon. He was in Jerusalem with those who had not yet been deported. In chapter 31, his discourse revolves around a New Covenant that will bring about the restoration of Israel. It speaks of a possible return to Jerusalem after a period of deportation. Is it the return from Babylon around 536 B.C., during the time of Governor Zerubbabel and High Priest Joshua , or is Jeremiah speaking of the return of Israel to the Holy Land at the end of times? At first glance, verse 14 leans towards the former option, as it mentions satisfying the priests with fatness. However, the Epistle to the Hebrews clearly states that Jesus is the final and complete sacrifice. Therefore, there is no reason for Jews who convert at the end of times to resume the service of animal sacrifices. So, if this text literally speaks of the resumption of animal sacrifices, it would point to the return to Jerusalem around 536 B.C.

However, the futuristic option emerges in the following text where there is talk of a collective conversion leading to an intimate knowledge of God (v. 34). Clearly, this description corresponds to the end of times, when a large part of the sons and daughters of Israel will recognize their Messiah (Rom 11:25-27). The text also depicts a socio-political stability where the land will never again be destroyed (v. 40). The Jews will then return to their land and multiply there (v. 27). God will ensure their return as He ensured their exile because of their disobedience (v. 28). This refers to the diaspora of 70 A.D. and the return of Israel to the Holy Land that has taken place since 1947 (partition of Palestine) and 1948 (creation of the State of Israel).

How then do we explain the sacrifices mentioned in verse 14? They would be sacrifices of the priests in the spirit of the New Covenant (Jn 4:24). Moreover, it is the soul of the priests that will be satisfied with fatness, according to verse 14, and not their bodies. We must conclude that the prophet here speaks of a spiritual worship and not of the reconstruction of the temple and the resumption of animal sacrifices. In the New Covenant, believers offer sacrifices of praise and their own lives to the Lord (Heb 13:15; Rom 12:1). The priests are no longer a separate class of people as in the Old Testament; all believers are priests (Rev 1:6; 5:10; 20:6). Therefore, it is in the context of the conversion of the Israelite people at the end of times that the proverb about sour grapes is cited by Jeremiah (vv. 29-30). The prophet emphasizes the difference between the conditional first covenant, which inflicted upon them the curses attached to their disobedience (v. 32), and the unconditional New Covenant through which the iniquity (*awvon*) of the fathers can be forgiven (v. 34). The prophet even says that this covenant will give them the ability to fulfill the Law because it will be deposited in their hearts (v. 33). Thus, a part of Israel has hardened, but a remnant will convert to the Christian faith at the end of times (v. 37). And on that day, there will no longer be any reason to speak of their apostasy.

> *And it shall come to pass, that like as I have watched over them,*
> *to pluck up, and to break down, and to throw down,*
> *and to destroy, and to afflict;*
> *so will I watch over them, to build, and to plant, said the LORD.*
> *In those days they shall say no more,*
> *The fathers have eaten a sour grape,*
> *and the children's teeth are set on edge.*
> *But every one shall die for his own iniquity:*
> *every man that eats the sour grape, his teeth shall be set on edge.*
> *Behold, the days come, said the LORD,*
> *that I will make a new covenant with the house of Israel,*
> *and with the house of Judah:*
> *Not according to the covenant that I made with their fathers*
> *in the day that I took them by the hand*
> *to bring them out of the land of Egypt;*
> *which my covenant they broke,*
> *although I was an husband to them, said the LORD:*
> *But this shall be the covenant*
> *that I will make with the house of Israel;*
> *After those days, said the LORD,*
> *I will put my law in their inward parts,*
> *and write it in their hearts;*
> *and will be their God, and they shall be my people.*
> *And they shall teach no more every man his neighbor,*
> *and every man his brother, saying, Know the LORD:*
> *for they shall all know me,*
> *from the least of them to the greatest of them, said the LORD:*
> *for I will forgive their iniquity,*
> *and I will remember their sin no more.*
>
> Jeremiah 31:28-34

Here, Jeremiah does not distinguish between guilt and victimization as Ezekiel does. However, he uses the same popular proverb as a metaphor to illustrate the damages resulting from Israel's sins and the promise of a new time to come. From verse 31 onward, Jeremiah explains why there will no longer be any reason to speak of the consequences of past sins. The messianic era will transform the social order to the point of canceling many of the consequences of sin. It is at this time that the Jewish nation will turn massively to the New Covenant, which offers radical forgiveness in Jesus Christ (v. 34). This is a dispensation different from the time in which Christians currently live. This new time will be an age of blessing and restoration. Satan will be bound for a thousand years (Rev 20:2).

Texts that make teeth gnash

The question that arises now is this: can these texts be used to prove that Christians cannot inherit the consequences of their fathers' misdeeds? I believe not. The text from Ezekiel simply recalls the principles of the Law: each is guilty of their own fault, but we can inherit the consequences of our fathers' sins. The text from Jeremiah announces the benefits of the messianic era, but we have not yet reached that time.

However, these texts are often the first to be cited by those who "grind their teeth" because of the theology of generational ties. I remember, for example, an impassioned email I received from my pastor in response to a very innocent question from me about the possibility that generational ties could exist. I was questioning some Scriptures and the stories people for whom we were praying shared with me. My pastor replied by quoting this proverb, which I found quite enigmatic. But he used it as if it were endowed with the absolute power to deliver the fatal blow to any hint of heresy that might arise from my timid question.

I now see that others, like me, have not seen anything in these texts that could attack the notion of generational ties. Moreover, our experience and that of many other Christians who have ministries of deliverance regularly confirm the existence of such ties. So I think those who use these passages to suggest that generational ties disappear with the New Covenant have not interpreted them in their context.

However, if this proverb about sour grapes does not destroy the idea that we can inherit generational ties in the New Covenant, other passages of Scripture explain how this New Covenant is more radical even now, during the period from the first coming to the second coming of Jesus. We will now explore these texts.

5
Propitiation

Paul, this great apostle to the nations, teaches that God had planned a new covenant even before the foundation of the world (Eph 1:4-5). He says this covenant is "in" Jesus Christ. This little word "in" is very significant. It means that God did not make his last covenant with us, but directly with His Son. Now, since Jesus is God, being Himself part of the divine Trinity, we must conclude that God made a covenant with Himself. And we are included in this covenant through our union with Christ. Nothing can be more solid than this! This covenant "in" Christ is perfect, complete, and definitive. By adopting us (Eph 1:5), God the Father unites us with His Son in whom we receive all the benefits of the New Covenant.

Like many covenants, this covenant had to be sealed by blood. Here, it is the blood of Christ himself that acts as a witness and guarantees the promise. He offered his life as a sacrifice for our sins.

In whom we have redemption through his blood,
the forgiveness of sins, according to the riches of his grace;
Ephesians 1:7

For by one offering
he has perfected for ever them that are sanctified.
Hebrews 10:14

This covenant requires no condition on our part because Christ has accomplished everything for us. He lived an exemplary life, without sin, perfectly fulfilling the essence of the Law (1 Pet 2: 22-24). Thus, He could die in our place since He Himself did not deserve death. The sacrifice of Jesus Christ on the cross is a perfect propitiation[45]. God offering Himself to appease His own wrath.

> *He that believes on the Son has everlasting life:*
> *and he that believes not the Son shall not see life;*
> *but the wrath of God stays on him.*
>
> John 3:36

> *Whom God has set forth to be a propitiation*
> *through faith in his blood,*
> *to declare his righteousness [...]*
>
> Romans 3:25

The effects of propitiation

The first coming of Jesus aimed at restoring the relationship with God. For this to happen, Jesus' sacrifice had to nullify the guilt resulting from our sins. Through Christ, we are reconciled with God, who sees us as righteous through the perfect sacrifice of Jesus (Rom 5:1, 10; Col 1:21-22). Propitiation covers the fault and makes God favorable. God acts by replacing our guilt with the righteousness of Christ:

> *For he has made him to be sin for us, who knew no sin;*
> *that we might be made the righteousness of God in him.*
>
> 2 Corinthians 5:21

> *There is therefore now no condemnation*
> *to them which are in Christ Jesus,*
> *For the law of the Spirit of life in Christ Jesus*
> *has made me free from the law of sin and death.*
>
> Romans 8:1-2

---

45 According to the Trésor de la langue française (TLF), propitiation is "a sacrificial act offered to a god to render him favorable, with the aim of obtaining expiation, forgiveness of sins."

The Cross has deprived the devil of the ability to keep Christians under his sway (Col 1:13). Indeed, Christ crushed the serpent's head as God had foretold to Eve (Gen 3:15). He "disarmed the rulers and authorities and put them to open shame, by triumphing over them in him" (Col 2:15). Satan can no longer accuse Christians before God (Rev 12:10). Jesus gathered humans to form his Church, which he protects from the realm of the dead (Mt 16:18). He has seated himself at the right hand of God (Col 3:1; Heb 10:12; 1 Pet 3:22), higher than any other spiritual authority in the invisible world (Phil 2:9-11). From there, he reigns until all are subjected to him (1 Cor 15:25; Heb 10:13) and all confess that he is the Lord (Rom 14:11). Christ is the *Shiloh*, announced by Jacob, who will rule the world (Gen 49:10) and who will put all his enemies under his feet (Ps 110:1-2).

The alliance in Jesus Christ also has the power to reverse the curses inherited from original sin and the iniquities of our ancestors. This is a very interesting fact for us. Indeed, he bore on the cross not only our personal sins but also all the curses that affect us (Isa 53:5; Gal 3:13). Among other things, Christ destroyed death (2 Tim 1:10), the ultimate consequence of original sin. If death reigned through Adam's sin, life is now spread to the multitude through the sacrifice of the one who could deliver us, Jesus Christ (Jn 14:6; Rom 5:15, 18; 1 Tim 2:5). By his death, Christ annihilated "him that had the power of death, that is, the devil; and deliver them who through fear of death were all their lifetime subject to bondage." (Heb 2:14-15). Whoever believes in him "has everlasting life, and shall not come into condemnation; but is passed from death to life." (Jn 5:24). In resurrecting, Christ gives humans the possibility of living eternally. Dr. James Maloney says that Christ paralyzed and rendered ineffective the principle of death[46].

---

46 Maloney (James), *Living Above the Snake Line,* Bloomington [IN], WestBow Press, 2015, p. 8.

Already, but not yet

However, we must understand that the Christian covenant occurs in two phases. It is only at the second coming of Christ that Christians will be fully rid of the presence of sin in their lives, of death, demons, and evil.

Regarding sin, there is already sufficient grace in Jesus Christ to give us access to a transformation of our way of living (Rom 12:2). The Spirit of Christ, which is the inheritance of believers, can subdue the sinful nature we have inherited and give us access to an abundant life (Jn 10:10). At the first coming of Christ, a transformation was initiated in the hearts. Indeed, God poured out the Holy Spirit on Christians who teaches and strengthens us so that we may imitate Christ in all our conduct (Jn 14:26; Rom 8:3-9; 1 Pet 1:15; 2:21; 1 Jn 2:27). Apostle John says that we do not sin if we abide in Christ (1 Jn 3:6), under the guidance of the Spirit. However, it would be an illusion to believe that we never sin (1 Jn 1:10). We do not always walk in the light that the Spirit brings into our lives. Sometimes we choose to follow our natural tendencies. The old nature of Christians still exists alongside the new. In short, we are "already" set apart (sanctified), but "not yet" perfect.

Similarly, those who believe in Jesus Christ have the promise of resurrection (Rom 8:29) and the promise of an imperishable and glorious body (1 Cor 15:42-50). It is already possible to taste the power to come (Heb 6:5). Christ himself healed many sick people, and he also entrusted to his disciples the mission of proclaiming salvation by healing the sick in his name (Mk 16:15-18). We still observe miracles today. However, we also experience illness and physical death. Thus, there is "already" a victory over illness, even if it is "not yet" complete. Peter Horrobin summarizes the situation thus:

> On the cross Jesus defeated Satan and gave us the opportunity of being freed from all the curses that he had put upon mankind,

"having become a curse for us" (Gal 3:13, RSV). Included amoung those curses were sickness and demonization[47].

Since Satan has already lost his rights, now, no principality can separate us from God (Rom 8:35-37). Moreover, Christ's disciples can already experience their authority over demons by casting them out (Mk 16:17). Yet, they are still present in the world. They have the power to tempt, lie, deceive, and harass. It is only at the end of time that the devil will be thrown into the lake of fire (Rev 20:10) and Satan will be crushed under our feet (Rom 16:20). In short, Christians "already" have authority over demons, but "not yet" the power to eliminate them everywhere and for good.

On the social level, Christ has also established conditions to break curses affecting the community, family, and work (Gal 3:13). Indeed, the Gospel has the power to abolish segregation and racial prejudices (Gal 3:28). It also calls us to renewed relationships between men and women, between rich and poor (Jas 1:9-10; 1 Jn 3:17). It has the potential to transform the dynamics between employers and employees (Col 3:22), husbands and wives (Col 3:18-19), parents and children (Col 3:20-21). History shows that the Church has played a significant role in establishing schools and hospitals. It has fought against slavery and contributed to the advent of human rights. Despite the mistakes it has made, it "already" gives a taste of a better world. But we do "not yet" live in the announced world where peace and justice reign perfectly.

Finally, Christ suffered to break the bad legacies that result from original sin and the iniquities of our ancestors. Here again, beneficiaries of the New Covenant can "already" pray to break them on the basis of Christ's propitiation (Isa 53:5; Gal 3:13; Tit 2:14; Heb 8:12; Heb 10:17; 1 Pet 1:18-19; 1 Jn 1:9) even if they are "not yet" able to eliminate their transmission once and for all. Christ died not only to cover by his blood the guilt

---

47   Horrobin (Peter J.), *op. cit.*, p. 90.

and consequences resulting from our individual sins but also the consequences of the sins of our ancestors.

In summary, believers have "not yet" entered the glory they aspire to, but they can "already" claim with authority, in the name of Christ: forgiveness of sins, healing, deliverance, transformed relationships, and liberation from generational ties. Christ's propitiation contains the necessary provision for all of this. And the situation is similar in each of these situations. Jesus' propitiatory sacrifice can intervene on the guilt of sin, on the corruption that weighs on all men (tendency to sin), and on the transmissible curses from generation to generation affecting our health, our families, and our work.

The theologian Gordon Fee describes all of this as "an eschatological tension between what we are and what we shall be[48]." At the moment, we only experience our liberation in part. It is only at the return of Jesus Christ that "the restituation of all things" will come (Acts 3:20-21). In the meantime, the whole creation groans and travails in pain and also awaits the manifestation of the sons of God (Rom 8:19, 23). However, we can already partially reflect the glory of God by fighting until death is finally abolished:

> *So when this corruptible shall have put on incorruption,*
> *and this mortal shall have put on immortality,*
> *then shall be brought to pass the saying that is written,*
> *Death is swallowed up in victory.*
> *O death, where is your sting? O grave, where is your victory?*
> *The sting of death is sin;*
> *and the strength of sin is the law.*
> *But thanks be to God,*
> *which gives us the victory through our Lord Jesus Christ.*
> *Therefore, my beloved brothers, be you steadfast, unmovable,*
> *always abounding in the work of the Lord,*

---

48 Fee (Gordon), *op. cit.*, p. 571.

> *for as much as you know*
> *that your labor is not in vain in the Lord.*
>
> 1 Corinthians 15:54-58

Asking to receive

Three things limit the effectiveness of Christ's propitiation. Firstly, we have just seen that the Lord acts in two stages. We "already" have forgiveness of sins. We "already" see some miracles happening. We observe restorations in our families and in the world. But it is "not yet" the New World that we will inherit with Christ.

Secondly, salvation is not universal. It is offered to all, but not all receive it favorably (Jn 3:16). The sons of the evil one spread evil in the world and in our families (Mt 13:38). Imagine then! If believers are sinners and have the potential to hurt their spouses and children, this is even more true for non-believers who practice occultism, blaspheme, and worship false gods! It is quite illusory to think that believers who are in the midst of such a jungle would not be influenced by these dark atmospheres! They will suffer the consequences of the sins of their fellow citizens and family members in this present generation.

Finally, the effect of propitiation is limited by a third point on which we will now dwell: heavenly realities can only materialize through faith. We must turn to God and ask with confidence to receive. Having a key in one's pocket is not enough to open a door; it must be used. Similarly, having promises is not enough; they must be claimed. This is a principle that Jesus and the apostles taught:

> *For every one that asks receives;*
> *and he that seeks finds;*
> *and to him that knocks it shall be opened.*
>
> Matthew 7:8

> *You lust, and have not:[...]*
> *yet you have not, because you ask not.*
> *You ask, and receive not,*
> *because you ask amiss,*
> *that you may consume it on your lusts.*
>
> James 4.2-3

There would certainly be more miracles and transformations in the world if more believers asked for them with faith in the Lord. The fall of the first humans came from doubt. Conversely, it is through faith and prayer that we can now have access to the full manifestation of the power of Christ's Cross.

There are many reasons why believers do not ask God to act. The text from James cited above tells us that sometimes we are not answered because we ask selfishly. But there are other reasons: laziness, lack of faith in the power and goodness of God, theological systems that teach that miraculous gifts no longer exist (cessationism), the false belief that all the effects of propitiation are automatically activated at our conversion without needing to ask. Peter Horrobin describes the danger of certain theological constructs in this way.

> Unfortunatyely, there are many people who are not happy with God. They construct their own caricatures of how God ought to behave and what He ought to be like, and then they worship the god they have constructed in their own minds. This is simply a form of idolatry, where men construct an idol of wood or stone, endue it with certain characteristics, work out a belief system associated with the idol and then live in fear lest they should offend the god they have made with their own hands[49].

We should ask God to act because all areas can be refreshed (Acts 3:19) by Christ's propitiation. Let's follow Daniel's example

---

49   Horrobin (Peter J.), *op. cit.*, p. 303. See Isa 40.18-20; 44.9-20.

who prayed about the iniquity of his fathers. It's interesting to note that Daniel prayed even though God had given a promise. Indeed, he began to intercede in the first year of Darius (Dan 9:1), around 539-538 B.C., when he read Jeremiah's prophecy about a return from exile after seventy years (Dan 9:2). According to biblical historians, he had been in captivity for about sixty-six years, following his deportation in 604 B.C.[50]. So, he must have prayed for about four years before the seventy years come to an end. He asked for the prophecy to be fulfilled, and he interceded for God to forgive his people.

I believe we must do the same: claim the benefits of our covenant, pray, and act in faith even if we have promises. This idea that the effect of propitiation is automatic particularly affects the issue of generational ties. Many believers are not even aware of such ties. Others think that their conversion automatically breaks the tendency to sin or the curses they have inherited from their ancestors in specific areas. So, they cannot ask to receive. The power of the Spirit is there, but it will not manifest until we move to ask God to act. The sick who were healed by Jesus did not sit comfortably waiting. They came to him. Our role is to ask, seek, and knock on the door of the Kingdom. Such an attitude is required not only for initial salvation but also for the Christian walk, for seeking healing and deliverance. The liberation from generational ties and spirits is no exception to this rule. There is no automatism.

Sometimes, we hear the testimony of someone who was instantly delivered from a bad habit at the moment of their conversion. It's a wonderful grace, but it's not the rule. Generally, you have to ask to receive. The only automatisms that result from our conversion are the forgiveness of sins and the promise of future deliverance from any curse, including eternal death. We are free in position,

---

50 Archer (Gleason L. Jr.), The vision of the seventy weeks, in Gaebelein (Frank E), *The Expositor's Bible Commentary,* Grand Rapids [Mi], collection CDs, Zondervan Publishing House, 1981.

but this is a promise and not a present reality. To walk in this reality, to experience "already" our liberation, we must claim by faith a portion of our future inheritance.

Some people say that it's up to God to decide their health and life events. Thus, we can read this comment from a French pastor: "Who am I to break a tie or break a curse? If God decides to curse, all I can do is implore grace[51]." But precisely, what is to implore grace? It's an active act of faith. Jesus and the apostles did not recommend passivity. Folding our arms and letting God decide our fate, under the pretext that He is sovereign, is not very spiritual. His sovereignty does not exclude the active participation of disciples who believe that God is good and answers the righteous (Jas 5:16-18). God also wanted to give his sons and daughters in Christ the authority to take possession of promises. Sometimes, fervent intercession leads to the authoritative declaration of divine promises. Ask, and you shall receive! Christ did not die in vain! He has conquered death and is victorious in all situations. The provisions are contained in Christ's propitiation. However, it is necessary to ask.

> *Till now have you asked nothing in my name:*
> *ask, and you shall receive, that your joy may be full.*
> John 16:24

> *And these signs shall follow them that believe;*
> *In my name shall they cast out devils; […]*
> *they shall lay hands on the sick, and they shall recover.*
> Mark 16:17-18

In summary, the work of Christ is a pure marvel. It liberates us perfectly from the consequences of the fall. This renewal is "already" initiated, but "not yet" completed. Christian hope is an

---

51 [On line] https://florentvarak.toutpoursagloire.com/faut-il-briser-les-liens-dheredite-episode-191/ (july 2020).

anticipation of the full realization of promises. But "already", we can join with the Son to ask Him for a pledge of the world to come, and thus inherit a portion of the benefits of propitiation today, among other things, to break generational ties.

6
The notion of links

In the early chapters of this book, I presented the idea that the tendency to sin and the consequences of the sins of ancestors are passed down from generation to generation. I emphasized that only the consequences, and not the guilt of the ancestors, are transmissible. We also saw that the New Covenant is superior to all others, and that Christ's propitiation can already liberate us from the burden imposed by demons, diseases, and generational ties. But this is not automatic. It must be requested.

In the next chapter, we will examine the practical aspects of generational ties. But first, we will discuss the general notion of ties and study difficult passages on this theme. Why do we use the term "tie" to describe the iniquity of our ancestors? A tie is an impediment in a person's life: the corruption of sin and the paralyzing effect of the curses that result from it. Indeed, some sins have an attraction force that cannot be resisted by the will.

> *For I delight in the law of God after the inward man:*
> *But I see another law in my members,*
> *warring against the law of my mind,*
> *and bringing me into captivity to the law of sin*
> *which is in my members.*
>
> Romans 7:22-23

James further describes the sequence of events from the strength of desire that precedes sin to the curses that follow it.

> *But every man is tempted,*
> *when he is drawn away of his own lust, and enticed.*
> *Then when lust has conceived, it brings forth sin:*
> *and sin, when it is finished, brings forth death.*
>
> James 1:14-15

Due to their fallen nature, humans are tormented by evil desires. They can resist them to a certain extent. But when they succumb to temptation, they break divine law, harm their neighbor, and inflict harm upon themselves. The unhappy sinner may sometimes seek to satisfy their soul by indulging in perverse pleasures, thus intensifying the vicious cycle. Escape habits may be formed, leading to dependence and dragging them into the downward spiral of spiritual, emotional, and sometimes physical death. This is how the sinner becomes bound to their sin and its consequences.

The fact that they are regularly hurt by others also leads them to try to prevent assaults. Psychological defenses serve this purpose, but this fortress is at the same time a prison. Phobia, avoidance, paranoid projection, rationalization, denial, repression are all means of avoiding suffering. These shrink their field of consciousness and prevent them from being in touch with their true emotions. The personality thus narrowed by defense mechanisms is imprisoned in this shell and does not understand that it is trapped within itself, separated from God, others, and their true self.

Rights and gateways

On this dark path, the fallen man will sometimes encounter a demon that will add to his torment. It should be noted that demons have real power over sinful humanity because Adam and Eve consented to collaborate with them. They have rights over unbelievers. They attack their thoughts, their emotions, and their bodies. They use their sins and their wounds, which act as moral and psychic fissures, to better infiltrate. To the bonds of sin are then added the bonds of the evil one.

What about those who believe in Jesus Christ now? We know that demons had no rights over Jesus Christ (Jn 14:30), because he was without sin (1 Pet 2:22) and he forgave readily (Lk 23:34).

Similarly, I believe that Satan has no more rights over the believer, because we are dead to sin and united to Christ (Rom 6:6). But we must not confuse "right" with "gateway." An image from one classic book of Frank and Ida May Hammond expresses this reality well. Demons would be squatters[52]. These occupants have no right to occupy a building. Yet, they do so illegally if the place is accessible. Similarly, demons do not have the right to invade believers, but they do so if they find an open door. A moral fissure (a recurring sin), a psychic wound (trauma, rejection), or a spiritual consent (occultism, vows) will serve as an entry point. It is therefore necessary to close these doors and to claim our rights. We have explained in the previous chapter that deliverance is included in Christ's propitiation, but it must be asked of God to receive it. We have the power to command demons to respect our rights, and the duty to protect the territory conquered by the Holy Spirit.

Put on the whole armor of God,
that you may be able to stand against the wiles of the devil.

Ephésians 6:11

In this last passage of Scripture, the original Greek word translated as "stand" is *histemi* (ιστημι), an extended form of the primary verb *stao*, which means to stand, to remain, to establish oneself. The image that Paul develops here is not that of a soldier invading new territory, but that of a soldier defending the territory he has already conquered. It is therefore essential to defend your whole being (body, soul, spirit) to prevent intruders from entering. This is the role of spiritual warfare. Even Jesus was attacked from the outside, but He resisted perfectly. He was tempted in all things (Heb 4:15). He knew how to discern and repel the enemy, even when it spoke through the mouth of His closest friend (Mt 16:22-23).

[...] Resist the devil, and he will flee from you.

James 4:7

---

52 Hammond (Frank et Ida Mae), *Les voleurs dans le temple*, Pomy [Suisse], Soteria, 1992, p. 10. (original : *Pigs in the Parlour*, 1973)

Fortresses

Those people who are bound by their sins, their consequences, and sometimes by demons, will develop a mentality that imprisons them. The apostle Paul speaks to us about fortresses of spiritual origin, not fleshly. They reside at the level of thoughts. They produce an ungodly or heretical mentality that distances us from the new life in Christ and from the knowledge of God.

> *For the weapons of our warfare are not carnal,*
> *but mighty through God to the pulling down of strong holds;*
> *Casting down imaginations,*
> *and every high thing that exalts itself*
> *against the knowledge of God,*
> *and bringing into captivity*
> *every thought to the obedience of Christ;*
>
> 2 Corinthians 10:4-5

This passage on fortresses conveys the notion of bondage very effectively. James Maloney indeed intersects the concepts of binding and loosing with that of fortresses. According to him, it is necessary to bind wrong mindsets to break down the fortresses and to loose right mindsets so that we can be free. For example, he suggests binding the antichrist spirit and loosing the divine anointing[53] (1 Jn 2:18, 22); replacing the spirit of slavery (dependence) with the Spirit of adoption (Rom 8:15); binding the spirit of error and loosing the Spirit of truth (1 Jn 4:6); binding conscious or unconscious fear and loosing strength (2 Tim 1:7); binding pride and loosing humility; binding jealousy and loosing love; binding laziness and loosing zeal; binding idolatry and loosing faithfulness to the true God; and binding the spirit of judgment and loosing grace[54]. A similar process involves stripping off sin and putting on Christian virtues (Eph 4:20-32).

---

53   The Christ is the Anointed One of the Lord; hence the idea that the spirit of antichrist opposes the anointing of God (His Spirit).

54   Maloney (James), *op.cit.* pp. 56, 63-71.

All the passages mentioned above describe the notion of bonds. The following story also does. Luke mentions in his gospel a woman who was crippled by Satan for eighteen years (Lk 13:16). This text is quite conclusive. We will analyze it in chapter 9 when we discuss the ministry of Jesus. Luke also speaks of sick people who are under the power of the devil (Acts 10:38). Finally, other passages from the Pauline letters speak of the traps of the devil that lie in wait for those who resist the Gospel, who have bad habits, or who worship money as a god (1 Tim 3:7; 6:9; 2 Tim 2:25-26). Bromiley comments on these passages as follows:

> The idea of gods and demons being equipped with traps and nets is ancient and widespread. The devil is not just an accuser but an active opponent who is at work to capture and destroy people[55].

Tying and untying

Some texts, more difficult to interpret than those preceding, are sometimes used to justify prayers aimed at binding and loosing people. These texts may seem appropriate at first glance since they use the words "bind" and "loose," and the Greek verb "loose" (*luo*) has various meanings that are very close to the idea of breaking bonds. For example, *luo* is used in Matthew 5:19 and John 5:18 to release a person from obligations related to the Law, and in 1 Corinthians 7:27 to indicate marital bonds.

> *Luo* is used for release from prison, the opening of what is closed, the destroying of foundations, and the putting off of fetters. The coumpound carry such senses as "to leave," "to loosen," "to relax," "to become slack," "to break off," "to untie," and "to part," i.e., those engaged in a struggle[56].

Two texts are often cited to support the notion of breaking ties with sin or with demons: Matthew 16:19 and 18:18. But does the

---

55 Bromiley (Geoffrey W.), *Theological Dictionnary of the New Testament*, Grand Rapids [MI], Eerdmans Publishing Company, 1985, p. 753.
56 *Ibid*, p. 543.

context justify such use of these passages? Some authors believe that these texts apply only to sins. This is what Leanne Payne (1932-2015), a pioneer in inner healing prayer who founded the ministry Pastoral Care and inspired many ministries including ours, believed. Madame Payne does not deny the existence of demons, however. But she prefers to cast them out rather than to bind them. She prayed to loose people from their sins, wounds, and false identities. For example, during a conference we attended, she gave the example of a transgender person who was "loosed" from their fantasies by confessing their sin[57]. Madame Payne emphasizes that not everything should be confused with demons.

> We may even, in our ignorance and zeal to help the person, name these things as demons and fancy ourselves as "binding" and casting them out. It is the *sin* that is to be bound and the *person* loosed from it. In contrast, the wounds are to be healed. If these have provided a place for demons to hide, we can easily enough expel them once thy are discerned[58].

However, not everyone seems to agree on what should be bound or loosed in the texts of Matthew. Since these texts are not very specific, some bind sin, others a human mindset, and still others demons. As for loosing, one may pray to loose virtue, will, or for the person to be loosed from sins or demons. Let's take a closer look at these texts:

> *And I say also to you, that you are Peter,*
> *and on this rock I will build my church;*
> *and the gates of hell shall not prevail against it.*
> *And I will give to you the keys of the kingdom of heaven:*
> *and whatever you shall bind on earth shall be bound in heaven:*
> *and whatever you shall loose on earth shall be loosed in heaven.*
>
> Matthiew 16:18-19

---

57 Annual Conference of Pastoral Care Ministries, June 2007, Wheaton College, Chicago [IL].
58 Payne (Leanne), *Restoring the Christian Soul through healing prayer*, Wheaton [IL], Crossway Books, 1991, p. 207.

> *Truly I say to you, whatever you shall bind on earth*
> *shall be bound in heaven:*
> *and whatever you shall loose on earth*
> *shall be loosed in heaven.*
>
> Matthiew 18:18

The context of Matthew 16 is Peter's confession of faith. He acknowledges that Jesus is the Christ, the Anointed One of the Lord, the royal Savior come to deliver Israel. Jesus confirms this revelation. He specifies that his kingdom is of heaven; and he promises Peter to give him the keys, so that Peter will have the authority to bind and loose. Based on these elements of the context, several theologians say that Peter's confession of faith gave him the authority to determine who will be accepted or rejected in the Church. Others liken the authority conferred to Peter to that of the rabbis who could impose or remove an obligation, determine if a student was bound to a rabbi's teachings or released, meaning dismissed from the school[59]. However, it should be noted that the apostles are not rabbis (Mt 23:8). Therefore, the fathers of the Church said that the use of the terms "bind" and "loose" here does not refer to the Law, but to the power to authorize and forbid[60]. It seems, therefore, that Peter received the authority here to bind and loose people for salvation. Moreover, it is through the hands of Peter that the first believers received the Holy Spirit. And it is the apostles who first transmitted the fundamental doctrines of Christianity.

However, this passage also mentions the gates of Hades (the realm of the dead). We can understand here that Peter has the authority to confer a salvation that liberates from death, the Church being the assembly of the redeemed. On the other hand, it is also possible that these terms designate the power of the world

---

59 Le Grand Dictionnaire de la Bible, Charols [France], Excelsis, 2004, p. 940.
60 Bromiley (Geoffrey W.), op. cit., p. 148.

of darkness[61]. We then come to the conclusion that the apostles have the power to overcome the works of Satan, to bind demons and to loose people who are oppressed by them. Furthermore, the revelation of Christ, which is at the heart of this passage, supports this interpretation, as the Greek word "Christ" means conqueror, ruler[62]. This passage would then say that the Church (the assembly of Christians) has the authority to break all types of bonds that affect it, including generational bonds.

The context of Matthew 18 is different. It deals with a process of reconciliation to follow when conflicts arise in the Church, including the exercise of discipline that can lead to excommunicating members when an attempt at reconciliation fails. We are thus talking here about binding or loosing people from the Christian community, from the communion of saints.

However, this situation is also linked to spiritual warfare. Indeed, the Bible says that divisions and heresies that arise in the Church are demonic (Jas 3:14-16; 1 Tim 4:1). Therefore, Christ gives the power to bind and loose where believers agree on a decision inspired by the Spirit. The parallelism between Matthew 16 and 18 then becomes more evident. The gates of hell will not prevail against the Church, neither to prevent it from proclaiming the pure Gospel nor to hinder its edification. Authority is given to its leaders both over humans and over demons who would seek to harm the Christian community. In short, these two passages concern bonds that affect the whole Church and not those that harm individuals in particular.

Let's now note the peculiarity of the verb tenses used in these two passages. Hammond, citing Williams, says that it is the passive form of the past participle[63]. The theologian Wayne Grudem, on

---

61 This interpretation is adopted by the Hammond couple, who cite as support the American Amplified version of the Bible. See : Hammond (Frank and Ida Mae), *op. cit.,* p. 124.
62 Maloney (James), *op. cit.*, pp. 2, 60.
63 Hammond (Frank et Ida Mae), *op. cit.*, p. 125.

the other hand, mentions that it is a periphrastic future perfect. However, they both arrive at the same conclusion.

It is best translated by the NASB, "Whatever you shall bind on earth shall have been bound in heaven, and whatever you shall loose on earth shall have been loosed in heaven." Several other examples of this construction show that it indicates not just a future action ("shall be bound"), for which a common Greek tense was available (future passive), but rather an action that would be completed before some future point, with effects that would continue to be felt[64].

Pastor Jack Hayford, founder of the Jack W. Hayford School of Pastoral Nurture, also comments on these verb tenses:

The past action is a clear reference to Jesus' consummate triumph through His cross, for it is there He secured in heaven all release of redemption's future workings. His "it is finished" becomes functional where it is welcomed and applied - both on earth in the visible realm and in the heavenlies in the face of all dark powers of fleshy and satanic origins[65].

Walking in the authority of the Lord, bearing the keys of his kingdom never gives us the right to predetermine what God wants to do. That is presumption of the first degree. [...] This is not the way God calls us to live. We are to move in response to Him, not the other way around[66].

In short, earthly judgments are based on what has already been accomplished by Christ, and will be confirmed at the Last Judgment. Our declaration will be fulfilled because God has already promised what we affirm. And this is the case for all the promises included in the propitiation of the Cross. The declaration has no power in itself. God does not give us a blank check to

---

64   Grudem (Wayne), *op. cit.*, p. 891.
65   Hayford (Jack), *Penetrating the Darkness*, Grand Rapids [MI], Chosen books, 2011, p. 102.
66   *Ibid*, pp. 116-117.

grant all our requests in advance. Nor do these passages say that God inspires us with prayers that he has designed in advance. We are not automatons. What they do say is that we cooperate with heaven, knowing our rights and privileges as heirs to the kingdom. We have the authority and the keys to claim what is already accomplished. For example, we can declare that the sins of a helpee who repents are forgiven. Another biblical text clearly states this.

> *Whose soever sins you remit, they are remitted to them; and whose soever sins you retain, they are retained.*
>
> John 20:23

This last passage sheds some light on how to pray. One biblical commentary says of this passage:

> Literally, it is: "Those whose sins you forgive have already been forgiven; those whose sins you do not forgive have not been forgiven." The first verbs in the two clauses are aorists, which imply the action of an instant; the second verbs are perfects, which imply an abiding state that began before the action of the first verbs. God does not forgive men's sins because we decide to do so nor withhold forgiveness because we will not grant it. We announce it; we do not create it. This is the essence of salvation. And all who proclaim the gospel are in effect forgiving or not forgiving sins, depending on whether the hearer accepts or rejects the Lord Jesus as the Sin-Bearer[67].

It is therefore very important not to go beyond the framework of what has already been accomplished by Christ's propitiation. Church leaders can only bind or loose what is already bound or loosed. We conclude from our analysis of Matthew 16 and 18, and John 20:23, that the authority of leaders extends both within

---

67 Tenney (Merrill C.), *The appearance to the disciples*, in *The Expositor's Bible Commentary, op. cit.* Vol. 9, p. 193.

(doctrine, discipline) and outside of the Church (evangelization). The primary focus of these texts is not directed towards binding or loosing individuals from individual oppressions. However, by extrapolation, we could say that Church leaders are mandated to loose all those who are captive by claiming the benefits of Christ's propitiation, since the Church stands against evil. The idea of binding demons and loosing them from their power would thus be in line with the thinking of the texts in Matthew.

Devilish ties

Two other difficult-to-interpret passages are sometimes used to justify interventions aimed at unbinding people from demons or binding these same entities. First, the word *luo* appears in John's first letter.

> *He that commits sin is of the devil;*
> *for the devil sins from the beginning.*
> *For this purpose the Son of God was manifested,*
> *that he might destroy (luo) the works of the devil.*
>
> 1 John 3:8

Some authors cite this text to support the idea that we can unbind people from demonic works. But this usage is dubious. Firstly, this passage speaks of "untying the works of the devil", not "untying from the works of the devil". Another Greek term should have been used to mean this[68]. What's more, it's important to place this verse in context. Here, the apostle John contrasts true believers who know the love of God (v. 1), the hope of eternal life (v. 2) and who have the knowledge of Jesus (v. 6), with another group of people who are of the world and who do

---

68 For example, in Heb 9:14, the conscience is cleansed "from dead works" (*apo ergon*). In Rev 9:20, other men did not repent "of the works" (*ek ton ergon*) of their hands. On the other hand, in 1 Jn 3.8, Jesus unties "the works" (*ta erga*) of the devil.

not live in union, through the Holy Spirit, with God and Jesus. In his commentary, Glenn W. Barker believes that these people have the characteristics of a protognostic group[69]. These people emphasized knowledge. For them, the human spirit was more valuable than the body. They therefore perceived the actions of the body as either vile or insignificant, leading to either asceticism or libertinism. Here, John seems to be describing this second group, who live without following the ethics of the Law (v. 3, 6, 9). Paul had also already faced people who asked him if one could continue to sin after receiving Christ's forgiveness (Rom. 6:1-2). His answer was an emphatic "no". In the same way, John exposes the contrast between good and evil, between God and Satan. He says that there is no sin in Jesus' life (v. 5), nor in the one who remains united to him (v. 6-7). In fact, Jesus came to take away sin (v. 5). Every Christian who follows Jesus tends to purify himself (v. 3). On the other hand, if we don't abide perfectly in Jesus, we sin and are then on the devil's ground (v. 4). John goes even further. He asserts that if anyone says we can sin as we please (the Gnostic thesis), he is of the devil (v. 8). And then he says that Jesus came precisely to *luo* the works of the devil.

John's primary intention here would therefore not be to speak of the deliverance of demonized believers. In context, the works of the devil are *luo* by the work of the Cross. Most Bible versions therefore translate *luo* here as "to destroy", a word that makes more sense in context. John's message would be this: "since Jesus came to fight all the consequences of sin, it is quite inappropriate to continue sinning as you protognostics profess!" Note that we can, however, just as we did with Matthew's texts, deduce, by extension, that the destruction of the devil's works through Christ's propitiation implies that believers can be freed from their

---

69 Gnostics as such appeared in the two centuries following John's letter. But the first Gnostic ideas may have been put forward as early as the first century. See : Barker (Glenn W.), 1 John, in *The Expositor's Bible Commentary*.

sins, the curses that flow from them, the demons that harass them and generational ties. But here, it would be an inference even further removed from the context than in Matthew's case.

A second passage whose exegesis is not straightforward is sometimes used in reference to binding demons. This teaching is reported in the three synoptic gospels (Mt 12:22-45; Mk 3:21-35; Lk 11:14-32). Here, Jesus speaks of binding the strong man before living in his house. Then there's the story of an evil spirit who goes out and comes back with seven more evil spirits because the house is empty (Mt 12:43-45; Lk 11:24-26). There are many interpretations of these passages. It's all the more difficult to choose one, given the different contexts of the three Gospels.

In Matthew, for example, Jesus is accused of casting out demons by the power of Beelzebul[70]. He replies that it would be illogical for a demon to cast out a demon, since they are not divided against themselves. Then he says that the strong man must first be bound. Jesus then talks about sin against the Spirit, the wicked hearts of mankind and the judgment of the Jewish nation. Only then does he address the issue of demons returning in power to the house.

Mark's gospel begins in the same way (illogical accusation, strong man, sin against the Spirit), then goes on to talk about his mother and brothers coming to get him. On the other hand, Mark doesn't mention the wicked spirit who goes looking for reinforcements, nor the Jewish nation. As for Luke's Gospel, we again move from the accusation to the argument of division, then to the strong man. Luke doesn't mention Jesus' words about the Spirit, but he does say, "He that is not with me is against me, and he that gathers not with me scatters." He then talks about the

---

[70] This term is probably a transliteration of the Aramaic *ba'al zebûl* meaning "the master of the dwelling", an image that refers to the demon who possesses a person. Djaballhah (Amar), *Paraboles aujourd'hui*, Québec, La Clairière, 1994, p. 145, note 49.

demon who leaves and returns with seven other, more wicked spirits. Finally, he ends his discourse by speaking of this wicked generation and the judgment of Israel to come.

It's not easy to put it all together. Do the returning spirits describe the hardening of Israel or are they teachings pertaining to the deliverance of individuals? And who exactly is this strong man? In a book on prayer, theologian Donald G. Bloesh believes that the strong man is Satan, and that the role of prayer is to resist him with faith in order to bind him and win souls for Christ[71]. However, Jesus isn't talking about intercession or evangelism here.

Another interpretation is that the strong man is a powerful spirit that must first be bound and expelled in order to be able to drive other spirits out of a person[72]. Those who support this personalized interpretation say that we must fill a person in whom we have just performed an exorcism, with the Spirit of God, in order to protect him or her from counter-attacks (the return of more evil spirits). They conclude, therefore, that it is risky to cast demons out of non-believers or weak believers who are not filled with the Holy Spirit.

These principles seem commendable to me, but is this really what Jesus was talking about here? Among other things, this interpretation disregards Jesus' discourse on the Jewish nation. It seems more plausible to me, in this context, that the strong man is Satan whom Jesus is about to bind by dying for our sins. However, if Israel does not convert, its spiritual condition will be worse than before. The house of Israel may have been cleansed

---

[71] Bloesh (Donald G.), *The Struggle of Prayer*, Colorado Springs [CO], Helmers & Howard, 1988, p. 133.

[72] There is only one spirit further on in the text. We can assume, however, that this spirit is given as an example, without excluding that there may be more than one.

of the works of the devil[73], but if it is not filled with the Spirit following conversion to Christ, it will be vulnerable to attacks from all kinds of evil spirits (religious, occult, etc.). This latter interpretation focused on history seems to me to be the main idea here. Isn't that precisely what happened?

Nevertheless, the metaphor of the cleansed house is still drawn from the practice of exorcism. Let us not forget that Jesus had just cast out a demon (Mt 12.22; Lk 11.14). We know that the Lord used everyday situations to express other ideas. Consequently, we can say that the examples mentioned were drawn from his experience of delivering individuals even though Jesus used them to teach something else.

In summary, it is undoubtedly wiser to avoid these difficult passages when teaching about individual ties, as their primary meaning is collective. However, if it is decided to use them, these texts are far from endangering the idea of praying to break ties, as they do not contradict an individualized application. However, we have seen many other passages that can be used to describe the hindrances (traps, snares, fortresses) caused by sins and demons. The coming of Christ to set the captives free is a scriptural certainty (Lk 4:18). Spiritual warfare is an undeniable reality. The New Testament affirms at least twenty-two times that the world of darkness and light are diametrically opposed; likewise, it is between Christ and the demons (2 Cor 6:15), between his thinking and that of the world, between the sphere of the Spirit and that of the natural man (Gal 5:17). Therefore, I believe that we can confidently pray to bind everything that Jesus promised to destroy on the cross: sin, curses, diseases, and demons. We can also release individuals from generational ties in order to release the work of the Spirit of God in their lives.

---

73 We can compare this image to the analysis of 1 John 3:8 which precedes: Jesus came to destroy the works of the devil.

7
Generational ties

We have just seen that ties, in general, constitute a trap or a net that ensnares people. A tie is also a burden that places a yoke on their shoulders; a spider's web that weaves around them; a series of obstacles that prevent them from reaching their goals. A tie limits people in their development. It can imprison them in a stereotypical way of thinking, or it can condition or create involuntary attachments. It can breed bad habits and insatiable desires. People affected by this spiritual reality feel paralyzed or controlled. A good example of this is a man who is madly in love with an adulterous woman; he feels guilty and would like to leave her, but he cannot resist her.

> *And I find more bitter than death*
> *the woman, whose heart is snares and nets,*
> *and her hands as bands:*
> *whoever pleases God shall escape from her;*
> *but the sinner shall be taken by her.*
>
> Ecclesiastes 7:26

There are all kinds of ties. In this chapter, I will speak more specifically about people affected by generational ties. We will also begin to discuss how to be delivered from them. A very important first principle is to obtain the consent and cooperation of the person being helped. For example, a person who does not want to give up an emotional dependency or a satanic pact cannot be released. However, it often happens that people are ambivalent, either because sins exert a strong attraction, or because a demon partially controls their will. The Hammonds insist that we should not force or manipulate people. However, these authors pray to bind the powers of darkness and free the will of those being helped[74]. Leanne Payne speaks of untying the will. Personally, in the absence of biblical text supporting the idea that we can "untie" it, I simply prefer to ask God to "strengthen" the will of an ambivalent person (Phil 2:13).

Once cooperation is established, we bring healing to the individuals. For this, we need discernment and to know what we are dealing with. Generational ties are not always sustained by evil spirits. However, they very often have a spiritual component, as they are mostly rooted in sins. For example, a racist attitude will be passed down through family and cultural education for generations. If these ties are not cut by appropriate prayers, they will tend to repeat from one generation to another. We observe this for attitudes (sexism or racism), as well as behaviors (violence, alcoholism, incest, adultery, prostitution).

Sometimes, a bad tie is created between two closely interacting generations, for example, between parents and children. Some of these ambivalent ties can be very destructive. Indeed, a relationship of control or codependency can persist until the parent's deathbed. This is contrary to God's plan (Gen 2:24). We must then separate the parent and their child. The caregivers, as Mrs. Payne says, will invoke...

> [...] the presence of the Lord, asking that His power and love enable us to discern, and then break, the bonds of oppression that enslave one person to another on a spiritual and emotional level. This oppression exists to varying degrees, but in some cases, it is as if the daughter's soul is "possessed" by that of the mother. This prayer certainly resembles an exorcism prayer, but it is solely aimed at delivering the daughter from the dominance of her mother and the "intrusion" of the latter into her very mind and soul. A young woman confided in me: "It is my thoughts that my mother violated!" Another

---

74 Hammond (Frank et Ida Mae), *op. cit.*, p. 34.

noted: "I can never escape my mother's presence, even if I am separated from her by hundreds of miles." This is truly a terrible bondage[75].

Mrs. Payne says that when the mother is "empty" and fills herself with the life of her child, the latter may feel pity and sadness toward her. They may also feel guilty about abandoning someone in such great need. Their emotions may therefore undermine their efforts at emancipation. This form of manipulation must be defused. The victim of this kind of mother must be liberated from the fear of not perfectly meeting all maternal expectations. They must be freed from the lie that this manipulation is a form of love.

They must be assured that only after accepting their freedom (a complete separation of their identity from that of their mother) will they be able to truly love their mother and have a healthy relationship with her – as a complete and mature person. As long as this step is not taken, a part of themselves is still immature, subject to the mother's law, and therefore susceptible to manipulation[76].

Psychologists use various terms to describe such situations. But in Christian circles, we often refer to these cases as "soul ties." These positive or negative ties occur between family members, friends, and sexual partners. When the souls of two people are linked, deep exchanges occur at the unconscious level. Evil spirits can also be transferred from one person to another[77].

Our focus here will be limited to toxic soul ties with a generational aspect. As we have seen, these ties can occur with a parent (biological father or mother, adoptive parents), as well

---

75 Payne (Leanne), *Crise de la masculinité*, Palézieux [Suisse], Éditions Raphaël, 1994, p. 125. Translated from French version by the author.
76 *Ibid*, p. 126.
77 Note that the term "soul tie" is also used by New Age practitioners, who perceive these ties as an enhancement of consciousness. However, we do not believe that these ties are always positive.

as with various members of the extended family. For example, a soul tie can form between a boy and a grandmother who takes on a parental role when the biological mother is an irresponsible teenager. We have also seen ties formed through identification with an ancestor. Elizabeth, for instance, shared the same name as her aunt, and she resembled her. Everyone in the family would remark, "Ah, you are just like Aunt Elizabeth!" However, her aunt had a strange mental illness, and, in turn, our subject ended up developing a neuropsychiatric degenerative disease that doctors could never diagnose.

Moreover, a soul tie may persist after the death of a parent when a person has difficulty grieving. In some cases, this person continues to maintain a relationship with the deceased by talking to them and making all their decisions based on the preferences of the deceased person. It should be noted that such a soul tie has been observed to open the door to an evil spirit that maintains a morbid atmosphere around the grieving person, especially when they pray to the deceased.

Curses that emprison

The curses that bind generations are usually linked to the sins or traumas of ancestors. They can also stem from less common causes. Curses have been spoken by ancestors against themselves or their descendants, or by external individuals against the family of ancestors. These latter curses are mediated by evil spirits. They exert a certain fatalism on external events, sometimes even putting lives in danger. For example, people may experience events such as accidents, bankruptcies, or social rejection.

Curses spoken by people who wished harm upon the family are sometimes accompanied by witchcraft practices aimed at casting spells on the descendants. For example, King Balak asked the seer Balaam to curse Israel (Num 22:12; 23:7; Deut 23:4). Even today, we see people from Africa or South America paying sorcerers to attack a person or a family. This also occurs between ethnic groups when there are racial tensions.

Curses spoken by our ancestors against themselves often stem from a poor self-esteem, such as men who believe they are worthless and will never succeed in life. This can have consequences for generations to come, as these curses can transfer a mentality and spirits of self-destruction and self-hatred.

The words spontaneously spoken by ancestors against their family lineage are often uttered by individuals who are angry. For example, Noah cursed his son Canaan because he had seen him drunk and naked. This curse affected all of Canaan's descendants (Gen 9:20-25). Nowadays, we see French Canadian children who have been regularly called *les petits maudits*[78] by their parents, or subjected to other recurring negative words. It is not surprising then that they end up living in an atmosphere of curse. Of course, psychological suggestion can partly explain the outcome for these children. But I believe that negative words also have a real spiritual impact (Prov 18:21).

But let's return to the most common situations: those linked to the sins and traumas of ancestors. In chapter 2, we have already discussed the consequences of shed blood. In our ministry, we have delivered people who inherited curses because their ancestors went to war. Sometimes, it is an abortion undergone by a grandmother that brings a curse on the descendants. We have also prayed for a lady who felt presences in the basement of her new house until it was revealed to us that a child had been buried there and our prayers had stopped the oppression.

The Word of God associates longevity with honoring one's parents (Ex 20:12; Deut 5:16; Eph 6:2-3). We can infer from this that premature mortality is sometimes a curse linked to a lack of

---

[78] Litteral translation would be : Litte cursed one, or Those damn kids.

honor towards parents. This is indeed an empirical fact observed by doctors and psychologists: poor relationships with our parents are the source of many ills. Do psychosomatic mechanisms alone account for the observed facts? Or is there not a tangible sin there, as the Bible describes it?

Sexual sins are also associated with curses. The Old Testament declares that homosexuality, adultery, bestiality, child sacrifice, and sexual relations during menstruation are practices that lead to the curse of the land (Lev 18:19-25). The apostle Paul states that the deliberate and continuous practice of various sins, including sexual sins, makes it impossible to enter the kingdom of God (1 Cor 6:9-10). Closer to our time, Pastor Derek Prince, whose teachings are well known in Christian circles, believes that illicit or unnatural sexuality is a source of curse[79]. We also observe several diseases and psychosocial problems affecting LGBT individuals more than others[80]. Similarly, fornication is another widespread sexual sin that has consequences for generations. However, nowadays, cohabitation has become the norm. Although we no longer call children born from these unions "bastards," they are still the product of a union that did not honor the marriage instituted by God (Heb 13:4). In prayer, the Lord has often shown fornication as a source of curse. Some individuals have even experienced physical manifestations when we prayed about this issue, suggesting the presence of a spirit of fornication.

Our society accepts unmarried teenagers having sex. Contraceptive failures are common at this age. The result is either abortion and bloodshed, or teenage pregnancy. Here are a few facts to quantify the situation[81]. Teenage mothers often

---

79 Prince (Derek), *Blessing or Curse : You Can Choose*, Grand Rapids [MI], Chosen Books, 1990, p. 76.
80 For a detailed discussion, see : Lizotte (Michel), *L'homosexualité, les mythes et les faits*, Montréal, Les productions ML, 2008, 305 p.
81 Genuis (S.J.), "The Dilemma of Adolescent Sexuality, Part III-Teenage Pregnancy", Journal SOGC, January 1994.

stop studying. They have more obstetrical problems, such as hypertension, iron-deficiency anemia, babies too big for the girl's pelvis and dystocia, premature labor, low birth weight, maternal death (2.5 times more), stillbirth (2 times more). They are often abandoned by their fathers. Most will live below the poverty line, and around two-thirds will receive social assistance. The majority will experience marital failure, regardless of their marital status. Researchers also know that the future of children born to these mothers is mortgaged compared to that of children born into a family with an adult mother and father[82]. They are more likely to have a limited IQ, more at risk of mental illness and suicide, learning disabilities and dropping out of school (2 times more), welfare dependency, foster care or institutionalization, physical and sexual abuse (3 times more), delinquency (4 times more), alcoholism and drug addiction. Finally, girls from these unions are at greater risk of repeating their mother's pattern by becoming pregnant before the age of 16 (7.5 times more likely)[83]. So here we have a situation that has been well documented both medically and socially. Few people see a link with the spiritual sphere. And yet, all these consequences stem from a culture of fornication which, as in the cities of Sodom and Gomorrah, is approved by the majority of citizens.

Many other curses resulting from various sins that have a generational impact are not reported in the Scriptures. But let's mention one last example on which the Bible insists. Francis MacNutt, renowned for his teachings and deliverance ministry, mentions that generational curses almost always stem from

---

Décarie (S.), "Adolescente et enceinte, quand l'échec contraceptif mène à la pauvreté", L'omnipraticien, April 1994.

82 Sylvester (C.), "Preventable Calamity", Progressive Policy Institute, 1994, pp.13-14. Quoting : Furstenberg (F), "The Next Generation : The Children of Teenage Mothers Grow up, Early Parenthood and Coming of Age in the 1990s", Rutgers University Press, 1992.

83 We can speak of a generational link here, since all the curses mentioned will be repeated from generation to generation.

occultism and idolatry practiced regularly by ancestors, especially if there were witches or Satanists in the family tree.

> The most memorable example I can think of is a woman who wanted prayer for a relatively ordinary problem: She had trouble being patient and was easily angered – a common human failing. She was a regular churchgoer; in fact, she taught Sunday school. But once we start to pray, her face changed into a snarling mask of rage. Worse yet, this ordinarily meek woman started speaking in an altered voice and insulting us. Fortunately, someone in our group had a gift of discernment and said, "This all started in a black mass said in England hundreds of years ago, when her family was consecrated to Satan." As soon as he said this, the spirit responded indignantly, "Who told you that?"
>
> [...] If someone in our ancestry did something such as consecrate the family to Satan, the disastrous results continue even beyond the fourth generation, until the curse is broken[84].

A complex reality

The concept of generational ties can explain many phenomena. It can also shed light on the failure of certain prayers that do not take this aspect into account. However, wisdom must be exercised. Just as we should not see evil spirits in every situation, but rather discern them when they are present (1 Cor 12:10; 1 Jn 4:1), it is essential not to attribute all the problems of a family to generational ties, but to identify them accurately if they are indeed the cause. Excess in this area leads to consternation. For example, Jacques Colant recounts on his webpage:

> One day, my wife refused a cup of coffee simply because she doesn't like it, never has, and probably never will. There was no other reason for her refusal. The person who had received

---

84 MacNutt (Francis), *Deliverance from Evil Spirits*, Grand Rapids [MI], Chosen-Baker, 2009, pp. 110-111.

us, and who believed in the doctrine of ancestral ties, instantly declared to her that she was surely held by an 'ancestral curse' [...]. Faced with such extravagance, really, one doesn't know whether to laugh or cry[85].

Not only are there not generational ties in every situation we encounter, but we also observe that curses do not always have an effect on the people they target. This inconsistency in the "cause and effect" of a curse can lead some to believe that curses are nothing more than vulgar superstitions. How can this be explained? The Bible says that a curse without basis has no effect (Num 23:8; Prov 26:2). If all doors are closed, evil words spoken against us will remain ineffective. Thus, the righteous who regularly confess their sins and claim Jesus' protection are shielded.

God's sovereignty also explains these variable outcomes. The case of Cornelius is interesting in this regard. He sought to know God, but he came from a pagan family that worshipped false gods. However, the Lord decided to show him grace. He did not automatically allow the curse that such ancestral practices were supposed to bring upon him to be fulfilled. Even today, some devout individuals living in very spiritually charged environments have no problems, while others, equally passionate about God, are affected and need to be delivered through prayer.

A third reason why curses may remain ineffective is that humans have some power to repel them. For example, Jesus was rejected, but He did not succumb to a sense of rejection or be overwhelmed by a spirit of rejection. Similarly, ten of the twelve spies sent to Canaan were filled with fear, while Joshua and Caleb chose to have a different spirit (Deut 1:22-38; Num 14:24). The same goes for us. If someone tells me that I am worthless and will fail my next math exam, I can reject this prediction and push it

---

[85] [Online] https://www.iltaime.com/single-post/2018/04/30/LES-LIENS-ANCESTRAUX (August 2020).

away. Conversely, I can accept it, and then it is very possible that this destructive word will come true[86]. Indeed, when we welcome a negative word, our consent not only affects our mentality but can also open the door to demons that then amplify its effect; and sometimes they are passed on to descendants.

Finally, a curse may go unnoticed if the demons carrying it remain inactive for a generation. In his deliverance ministry, Peter Horrobin observes that generational spirits do not manifest in every generation. However, they must have been transmitted to the unaffected generation before reaching the next one[87]. This does not make the issue of generational ties subjective. This situation is comparable to the transmission of a physical disease such as type II diabetes, which is often seen in grandparents and grandchildren, skipping the middle generation. However, specific criteria are applicable for diagnosing diabetes. Similarly, the caregiver must take a rigorous approach to discern or deduce the presence of generational ties based on specific criteria, even if manifestations of ancestral ties are inconsistent in the family tree. We will describe these criteria. But before that, we will talk about the reality of demons.

---

[86] Note that the more important a person is to us, the more their words can affect us. Therefore, children are particularly vulnerable to the words of their parents. Furthermore, they have not yet developed the judgment and strength needed to push back against adults' assertions about them. Thus, they generally believe that what adults say is true, and negative comments about themselves can become ingrained in their identity.

[87] Horrobin (Peter J.), *op. cit.*, p. 462.

8
Spirits and demons

Many religions, including Christianity, believe in the existence of demons[88]. The apostles witnessed that Jesus, in addition to dying to obtain the atonement of our sins, healed thousands of sick people and drove out a multitude of demons.

> *When the even was come,*
> *they brought to him many that were possessed with devils:*
> *and he cast out the spirits with his word,*
> *and healed all that were sick.*
>
> Matthew 8:16

This historical fact finds an echo in the prayer that our Lord taught to his disciples, the "Our Father":

> *[...] And forgive us our debts,*
> *as we forgive our debtors.*
> *And lead us not into temptation,*
> *but deliver us from evil.*
>
> Matthew 6:12-13

In this passage, the notion of being delivered from the evil one is different from that of forgiveness of sins. Jesus made two separate requests. Additionally, the Greek word translated as "evil" clearly refers to a demon, likely Satan himself, and not just the concept of evil. Therefore, we need to be forgiven for our sins, but also to be delivered from the bonds in which the evil one holds us captive. How should this be done in practice? What is the difference between a spirit and a demon? How do

---

[88] For a more in-depth discussion on the existence of demons, refer to my book *Espoir pour l'âme et l'esprit, le miracle de la guérison intérieure*, pp. 35-47.

they act? What role do they play in generational ties? Can spirits be transmitted by our ancestors? If so, in what way?

Knowledge of the enemy

We need to understand the enemy if we want to effectively combat it and take measures to protect ourselves. According to the understanding of rabbis and Church Fathers, God created the angels, and a portion rebelled to form the kingdom of darkness. Then, they were cast down to earth (Rev 12:7-9). The Bible specifies that demons are structured in hierarchy (Eph 6:12). The chief of demons is the devil, a Greek word meaning "the accuser" (Rev 12:10). He is also the evil one, inherently wicked, and the source of evil (Eph 6:16). He is referred to as Satan, an Aramaic word meaning "adversary". He opposes God by stimulating humanity's rebellion (Eph 2:2), while also fighting against His people to prevent conversions (Mt13:19; Acts 13:6-10, 16:16-18; 1 Thess 3:5) and corrupting sound doctrine (1 Tim 4:1; 2 Pet 2:1). The whole world is under his power (1 Jn 5:19), for he is the prince of this world (Jn 12:31). He even has the ability to redistribute wealth to those who obey him (Mt 4:9; 6:24). He can perform miracles and inspire false prophecies (Mt 24:24; 2 Thess2:9).

The subordinate demons, on the other hand, conceal their true nature (2 Cor 11:14) and work in secrecy (Jn 3:20; Eph 5:11-13). They manipulate thoughts (2 Cor 10:4-5; 1 Jn 4:1-3). Like their master, they are liars, murderers (Jn 8:44), seducers (2 Thess 2:9-10), depraved, and impure (Mk 1:23). Some are more wicked than others (Mt 12:45).

The Bible uses the words "demon" and "spirit" to describe these supernatural beings. It is not always easy to distinguish between spirits and demons. The term "spirit" could be the generic term because God and the good angels are also spirits who do not have bodies (Jn 4:24; Heb 1:14) just like Satan (Eph 2:2).

However, we see texts where both words are used interchangeably to refer to the same spiritual being. For example, in Luke 9:42, we read: " And as he was yet a coming, the devil[89] threw him down, and tare him. And Jesus rebuked the unclean spirit, and healed the child, and delivered him again to his father". Here, the two words seem synonymous. Similarly, these terms alternate in Mark 5:12-13: " And all the devils sought him, saying, 'Send us into the swine, that we may enter into them'. And immediately Jesus gave them leave. And the unclean spirits went out, and entered into the swine."

However, there are authors who distinguish demons and spirits. According to some Satanists and certain Christians, a demon would be a grouping of spirits[90]. However, we cannot conclude that spirits are less powerful entities than demons, since Satan and God are spirits.

The biblical language often gives the impression that the word "spirit" is used to describe the function or specific mission of a demon. For example, there is mention of a spirit of lying in a context where it is very clear that it refers to a fallen angel pushing false prophets to lie (2 Chron 18:20-22). There is also talk of a mute and deaf spirit (Mk 9:17-25) and a spirit of divination (Acts 16:16), which are specialized in these areas.

The puzzle becomes even more difficult to solve when we consider biblical passages that may refer to a mental state in humans. For instance, when there is mention of a spirit of pride (Prov 16:18), of bondage (Rom 8:15), of slumber (Rom 11:8), of timidity (2 Tim 1:7), or of error (1 Jn 4:6), are we describing simple human mentalities or demons accentuating these mentalities? The entirety of Scripture shows that the human spirit can come into contact with spiritual beings and undergo their influence.

---

89 In the original Greek, the word "devil" is "δαιμόνιον" (*daimónion*), which means a demon.
90 Horrobin (Peter J.), *op.cit.* p. 98.

We know that the Spirit of God can produce a mentality of life (Rom 8:2; Rev 11:11), of gentleness (Gal 6:1), or of wisdom and revelation (Eph 1:17). The result of this influence is that a disciple of Christ can then produce the good fruit of the Spirit, which is love, joy, peace, long-suffering, gentleness, goodness, faith, meekness and temperance (Gal 5:22-23). Furthermore, the influence of evil spirits can lead to destruction (Lk 9:55), slander and division (Phil 1:17; Jas 3:14-16), or heresy (1 Jn 4:1, 6).

Despite some ambiguity in scriptural vocabulary, it is clear that supernatural spirits, whether good or evil, influence us. It is noteworthy that the Bible still holds humans responsible for their decisions. Even the non-believer, though blinded by Satan, will be judged based on the response given to God when, in His providential grace, the Holy Spirit reveals His existence to them through Creation or the message of the Gospel. Moreover, humans have the ability to resist evil spirits. Especially the Christian, as they receive the help of the Holy Spirit to discern where their thoughts, desires, and sometimes even the voices they hear come from. A Christian must therefore recognize the influences, resist the bad spiritual sources, and only welcome the good ones.

Some authors believe that the Holy Spirit exclusively dwells in the spirits of Christians and that demons only inhabit the body or soul. It is difficult to find irrefutable biblical evidence for such claims. Personally, I believe that the human spirit is a territory of revelation and a battlefield where a war takes place. The stakes are to maintain truth and combat error (2 Cor 10:5).

Demonization

Here's how evil spirits work. We've explained that demons use traumas suffered or certain sins committed voluntarily as entry points. Evil spirits bearing the names of these traumas or sins can then gain access and exacerbate wounds and tendencies of the old self.

Some passages of the Bible illustrate this dynamic well. For example, anger is a normal emotion in the face of certain injustices. Jesus himself sometimes felt righteous anger. However, when we harbor anger or when the cause of our anger is unjust, it produces bad fruit like gossip or violence. There are people who are possessed by a smoldering anger accompanied by evil thoughts. And just as adultery comes from lust (Mt 5:27-28), murder is often conceived in anger (Mt 5:21-22). If a person does not control this destructive evil when it approaches to tempt them, it is this evil that will dominate them, as was the case for Cain who became angry and killed his brother (Gen 4:3-8). That's for the emotional and moral dimension. But the apostles go further and speak of a diabolical component in their teaching. Paul says that harboring anger can give the devil a foothold (Eph 4:26-27). The epistle of James also speaks of a spirit of contention that is diabolical (Jas 3:14-16). These passages thus describe a gradation from normal anger, to a chronic tendency to get angry, and finally, to destructive anger. The more the human spirit voluntarily gives access to the sin of anger, the more there is a risk of opening the door to a demonic power that will accentuate the tendency to sin in this specific area. The affected person, or, let's rather say infested, will then more easily lose control and risk committing deplorable acts.

Other unrestrained sins follow this pattern and open the door to a demon. Take the case of a man who consumes pornography without resisting it. He thus succumbs to evil. A demon could come and exacerbate his vice, pushing him towards more serious sins such as prostitution, rape, or pedophilia. This phenomenon is described by scientists as a state of addiction and habituation whereby a stronger sensation is required to generate the same pleasure. Thus, David Scott summarizes in an impressive work the conclusions of over five hundred studies on pornography. He summarizes the effects of pornography in six points: 'hard' pornography is not the only one that is harmful ('soft' pornography is also harmful to all individuals); pornography desensitizes the follower; it creates a phenomenon of addiction; it leads to a deterioration of the marriages of affected individuals; it increases the risk of sexual crimes among predisposed individuals; finally, pornography increases the risk of other criminal acts such as drug consumption. But how does this addiction occur? Is it purely a biochemical phenomenon in the brain? Is it a particular personality disorder? Or do we accept that, in some cases, the influence of a demon can drive a man to commit perverse acts? I think that the account of several sexual crimes leads us to the conclusion that there are sometimes demonic influences. The spirit of fornication (*porneia* in Greek) is an impure spirit attached to sexuality. It fosters a mentality and behavior of a person who does not respect the framework of marriage for their sexual activities.

The activity of evil spirits may well explain facts for which science provides little explanation. For example, on two occasions I have counseled men addicted to pornography who reported an intense desire to have sexual relations immediately upon making eye contact with a woman driving a car at a good distance. According to my clients, these women would simultaneously manifest the same desire by gesturing with their hand. Even though the men in question were born again, they had great difficulty in resisting this temptation. Is it possible that these two men and these two women had spirits of fornication that allowed them to easily identify each other, to attract each other mutually, and to cause such a loss of control?

I have also been consulted as a doctor by a woman who sought my help because she felt compelled to sleep with every man, and did not understand why. I could also feel a spirit of seduction acting upon me. Furthermore, she had chosen to consult late on Friday evening without an appointment. She was my last client. My secretary was about to leave and leave us alone. I felt uncomfortable explaining to this secretary why she should stay, especially as she had pressing obligations. I then remembered a verse that I had memorized and had endeavored to recite the previous week: 'There has no temptation taken you but such as is common to man: but God is faithful, who will not suffer you to be tempted above that you are able; but will with the temptation also make a way to escape, that you may be able to bear it.' (1 Cor 10:13). So I cried out to God for help. And miraculously, a child suffering from a severe asthma attack appeared just as my secretary was about to lock the door! I asked my client to come back during my next shift. I thought I could prepare myself in prayer and that there would be a rush at the clinic during the day. She agreed, but as she walked out the door, she struck a very sexy pose and gave me a very seductive look. I know that some people will persist in seeking only psychological explanations for this kind of situation. But it will still be difficult for them to explain God's intervention in response to my prayer: in twenty-three years of medical practice at this clinic, it's the only time that a child has presented with an asthma crisis on a Friday night at ten o'clock! Normally, at that time, people know the clinic is closed and they go to the emergency rooms of hospitals.

Physical or psychological traumas can also open the door to evil spirits. For example, in our ministry[91], we encounter people who have spirits of rejection. They constantly feel excluded. Sometimes, the spirit even acts on the surroundings and triggers exclusion. Our approach is to ask the Lord to reveal the origin of the problem so that we can pray better. The Holy Spirit sometimes leads us back to events surrounding birth. Some helped individuals were not desired by their parents. In other cases, we have seen that the parents were simply indisposed on the day of birth. Yet, the little newborn baby perceived this lack of welcome, and it had long-term consequences. Shedding light on these things allows the person being helped to better understand and objectify the facts with adult eyes. The most important thing is for them to renounce the mentality of rejection because this mentality acts as

---

91 For more details on our approach to inner healing prayer, please refer to chapter 10 of this volume, and to my book *La guérison intérieure – Manuel de formation*.

an interpretation filter, like a cognitive and emotional mold that distorts their perception of relationships with others.

When a demonic spirit of rejection has used this trauma to enter the child's life, it must be cast out, and then life declared over the little baby while we are praying with the Lord, recalling the moment the injury occurred. We also declare that God desired to welcome this little child into the world, even if his parents were not disposed to do so at that time. Some helped individuals even relive childbirth by seeing themselves welcomed into the arms of God the Father, even before we prayed for it.

Generational spirits

If evil spirits accentuate the sins or traumas of the individual in their own life, generational spirits accentuate the sins or traumas of ancestors in the lives of their descendants. The example mentioned above of acquired rejection at birth shows us that evil spirits can be acquired very early. This can even occur during pregnancy. It is well known that the child hears sounds. Even if they do not understand their parents' language, they will perceive the emotional and spiritual atmosphere around them as their parents discuss, for example, considering abortion. Moreover, they will feel their mother's pulse quicken during a dispute between spouses. This can evoke fear. These events can serve as an entry point for spirits of rejection or fear, which could later cause generalized anxiety, without anyone knowing why.

Strictly speaking, a spirit acquired in the mother's womb should be called a "congenital spirit." To be classified as generational, a spirit must first have harassed the parents or grandparents. The only distinction between a generational spirit and a personal spirit is that it is transmitted from one generation to another. The entry point is then found in the ancestors. Generational spirits then work to embed the sins (anger, fornication) and traumas (rejection, fear) of the ancestors into the family.

Generational spirits of fornication and adultery, for example, will lead to a tendency in the extended family to engage in sexual relations outside of marriage. They will bind descendants to this immoral habit. A word of authority is needed to break this dependence. So, when Jesus said "go and sin no more" to the adulterous woman or to other sinners, I don't think he was asking the person to stop committing sins absolutely. That's impossible for anyone! I believe he was talking about not reproducing certain sins, whether they were caused by generational ties or not. I cannot prove it, but I believe that this word from the Son of God made the person capable of obeying. "For he spoke, and it came to be; he commanded, and it stood firm" (Ps 33:9). Indeed, God helps us to accomplish what he requires. His word has a liberating effect. That's why, in my opinion, this word of Jesus had the power to deliver the person from a bond of dependence, and even to cast out a generational spirit.

The situation is different for spirits linked to occult practices carried out by ancestors. These demons are not connected to human attitudes but are mandated to carry out curses or maintain pacts that have been made with Satan.

Individuals who have ministries of healing and deliverance accumulate numerous experiences that demonstrate the existence of generational spirits. For example, Peter Horrobin observed that spirits can cause the repetition of the same patterns from generation to generation for nightmares, narcissism, premature mortality, and accidents[92]. He also reports that generational spirits of adultery push married couples or couples living in common-law marriages to be unfaithful from generation to generation[93]. He mentions generational spirits causing physical infirmities as a result of occult practices, traumas, sexual sins (fornication, incest), or parental domination[94]. He successfully cast out spirits

---

92   Horrobin (Peter J.), *op. cit.*, pp. 330, 333, 335, 415.
93   *Ibid*, p. 385.
94   *Ibid*, pp. 105, 336, 346-347, 382, 410.

of seasonal depression attributed to sun and seasonal worship by ancestors[95]. He has seen spirits causing heart diseases in descendants of people who hardened their hearts against God[96]; spirits causing homosexuality, cross-dressing, and gender disorders when ancestors practiced homosexuality[97]; and mute spirits in descendants of people who participated in satanic rites that cursed the tongue of anyone revealing the sect's secrets or seeking to leave it[98].

Derek Prince reported discovering the reality of evil spirits when about ten people were delivered from mute and deaf spirits in a single evening in Pakistan[99]. I myself observed a large number of deaf individuals during a missionary trip to Brazil, a phenomenon many attributed to poorly treated ear infections. However, upon reading these various deliverance testimonies, I am now inclined to believe that many of these individuals could have had generational spirits in these places where many ancestors practiced witchcraft. It was wonderful to see these people healed in response to our prayers.

According to Horrobin, generational spirits can be transmitted to descendants at any time[100], but they are more often transmitted at the time of the parents' death[101]. In some religions that worship ancestors, such as Taoism, certain rites are even practiced that give consent to spirits from their followers. The aim is to receive

---

95 *Ibid*, p. 320. According to Horrobin, a spirit may be at fault here, even if there is an excess of melatonin observed. The answer to prayer is the proof of this.
96 *Ibid*, p. 326.
97 *Ibid*, pp. 389, 395.
98 *Ibid*, pp. 151-152.
99 Prince (Derek), *Pulling down Strongholds*, New Kensington [PA], Whitaker House, 2013, pp. 11-12.
100 We have already mentioned that a poor relationship with a parent, such as an abusive relationship (bad soul tie), can serve as a channel (entry point) during the parents' lifetime. Horrobin also observes this.
101 Horrobin (Peter J.), *op. cit.*, pp. 188, 346, 417.

the strength of the ancestors[102]. Moreover, in such a religious context, the paranormal knowledge of individuals' past lives, often attributed to the phenomenon of reincarnation, could very well be explained by the transfer of generational spirits[103]. Therefore, these practices should not be taken lightly. That's why I am saddened to see that several Western films adopt these ideas in a romantic context, for example, in a scene where one gazes at the stars while invoking our ancestors!

In 2013, I experienced a situation that convinced me of the existence of generational spirits. Alongside my medical career, I became an assistant pastor in a Pentecostal church. The senior pastor asked me to take charge of a teaching and healing program called *Cleansing Stream Ministries*. For this, I had to attend training in the province of Ontario with some members of my church. We received brief instructions and quickly moved to practice because a conference followed immediately after our training. We were paired with a minister who showed us how to care for people coming forward to receive prayer after the teachings they received. The final teaching of the conference was about the spirit of death and its effects in people's lives. The prayers accompanying this teaching consisted of choosing life and renouncing any thought of death, breaking the effect of death-spoken words on our lives, and casting out any spirit of death. The conference was now over. I was resting when someone came to get me, saying that my wife needed me. The non-verbal cues from this person indicated that the situation was urgent. So, I followed the messenger who led me backstage to a sort of dead-end corridor where five people had gathered, including my wife.

One of the volunteers had asked for prayer because she had been affected by the last workshop but hadn't been able to attend. The four people who tried to help her had followed the usual

---

102 *Ibid,* pp. 188, 529.
103 *Ibid,* p. 196.

procedure and cast out a spirit of death. That's when the young woman became agitated. That's when my wife asked for me to be called to join their group. When I arrived, the woman was standing, crying, and looking at the ground. If I tried to approach, she would violently bend forward and recoil. They briefed me on the story. She said she felt ugly and couldn't make love to her husband since giving birth a year ago. As a doctor, I asked her a few questions that seemed to rule out a physical problem. Moreover, her personal physician had told her that everything was normal during her examination. Her symptoms didn't seem to come from postpartum depression according to her doctor, she said, and according to her husband, who was one of the people present.

We then sought to discern the problem by asking questions to God and listening for the answer in our spirits. My wife, who has prophetic gifts, received that it was related to her mother. She asked the young woman if her relationship with her mother was good. Again, everything seemed fine. But at that moment, the husband mentioned that this woman's mother had the same problem, as did her grandmother. All three of them felt ugly. So, we cast out a generational spirit of death, rather than just a personal spirit of death. However, this simple difference in naming had an immediate effect. This young woman was completely changed in an instant.

This story was all the more impressive to me because I didn't have much faith while praying. Indeed, this young woman had a lot of acne. Moreover, she was disabled. To be honest with you, while praying, I thought to myself that she had good reasons not to find herself beautiful! But after her healing, she was so different. She started smiling. She was radiant, cheerful, and funny. I now found her very flirtatious! Then, this woman and her husband mutually forgave each other for the words exchanged during this difficult year. And we left, delighted with our experience. So, I came back from Ontario convinced that generational spirits really exist and that it is important to differentiate between personal spirits and generational spirits when we pray.

Discerning spirits

The gift of discerning of spirits (1 Cor 12:10), activated during times of listening to the Holy Spirit, is very useful for determining whether a demonic spirit is present or not. This gift operates in different ways. I have known people who saw shadows or points of light, while others saw snakes. The Bible possibly describes how this gift operates when it says that we will tread on serpents and scorpions (Lk 10:19). But regardless of the manner in which it operates, the important thing is that it enables the identification of spiritual realities behind the perceived images. Generally, people with this gift eventually understand what their visions, intuitions, or sensations refer to. Is it a human spirit, a personal spirit, or a generational one? Those with this gift of the Spirit are also often able to discern the names of spirits and how they entered. They can often determine the rank of a spirit. What a magnificent gift!

However, this gift is not infallible. When a person with this gift does not see a spirit, we cannot assert that there is none. Sometimes, another person with the same gift will discern one. Furthermore, it is useful to have other criteria since we cannot always work with someone who has this gift. For example, we may suspect a demonic presence when our prayers have had no effect in previous sessions or when the individual being helped suffers from multiple oppressions from various external sources. Observing physical manifestations is also an indication[104]. We can name the spirit based on the sin it urges to commit or the trauma it perpetuates. Finally, we may suspect that the spirit is generational when the life of the individual does not provide us with an event likely to have triggered the problem we are seeking the origin of, or when several family members report similar phenomena.

---

104 This last topic, however, exceeds the scope of this book. These signs and symptoms are mentioned in my *Manuel de formation,* p.154.

Without the gift of discernment, it is almost impossible to determine precisely how a demon gained access to the lives of ancestors, as the situation is always more complex for generational spirits. Were there unconfessed sins or unforgiven hurts suffered? For example, an abortion or a suicide attempt could open the door to a generational spirit of death. An ancestor who suffered sexual assault may have experienced anxiety caused by a spirit of fear. These spirits can then be passed down to descendants. When this happens, they can affect not only the behavior of the afflicted person but also their environment and the people around them. They can also be passed on to subsequent generations. This explains why accidents, assaults, or unfounded fears may repeat from one generation to the next.

When multiple doors are opened, many spirits can lodge in the same person, thus creating a fortress that partially controls the victim's thoughts. In these cases, it is not always easy to identify all the demons. We could cast out the spirits we have identified and command all others associated with them to leave. Furthermore, sometimes clarity comes through prayer.

Finally, it is worth noting that the practice of occultism and sorcery are powerful entry points for various spirits that can be transmitted to descendants. We may see, for example, spirits of infirmity, lust, divination, and sorcery. Sorcery is common in most countries around the world. And we observe that believers are affected even if these practices were only carried out by their ancestors.

> Because the spirits of the occult can enter a person through ancestry, and because a spirit of witchcraft can come down through the generations, it will continue to be passed down until that particular ancestral connection is broken and any spirit of the occult is cast out. At times we pray for an entire family – grandparents, parents, children – asking Jesus to cleanse the bloodlines and free the family from any spirits that

have been passed down. This is usually done peacefully and easily when the family in this generation is doing their best to live Christian lives and have not themselves been involved in the occult[105].

Exorcism and baptism

If Christians can be affected by personal and generational spirits, it is easy to conceive the enormous task that pastors face in healing and delivering their flock. Could there be less laborious means than individual deliverance? Some pastors[106] and laypeople[107] are rediscovering today the possibility of praying for deliverance during water baptism. Indeed, it is a historical fact that deliverance has been practiced during baptisms among both believing adults and children since the beginning of the Church. Hippolytus of Rome (A.D. 250) reports that exorcism was practiced during the baptism of all Christians[108]. Similarly, the Seventh Council of Carthage (A.D. 276) ordered exorcism by the laying on of hands, followed by re-baptism for those who had caused divisions and desired to return to the Church[109]. Lutherans abandoned the practice of exorcism during baptism only in 1916, but this practice resumed in the 21st century[110]. Finally, the Roman Catholic baptism still includes prayers of exorcism aimed at purifying the baby from any influence of the kingdom of darkness[111]. Francis MacNutt, who was a Dominican

---

105 MacNutt (Francis), *op. cit.*, p. 223.
106 Yves Lanel [online] https://www.youtube.com/watch?v=yld0Q-OaxYc (30 sept 2020).
107 Torben Søndergaard [online] https://www.youtube.com/watch?v=p55AMpE9jkA (30 sept 2020).
108 MacNutt (Francis), *op. cit.*, p. 137.
109 Horrobin (Peter J.), *op. cit.*, p. 251.
110 Clark (Randy), *op. cit.*, p. xix.
111 [Online] https://liturgie.catholique.fr/accueil/initiation-chretienne/le-bapteme/bapteme-des-petits-enfants/13303-lexorcisme-dans-le-rite-baptismal/ (août 2020).

before leaving the clergy to marry and found a healing ministry, says this:

> The idea behind the infant baptism is not only to fill the baby with God's life from the very beginning, but also to protect him from evil. The Roman Catholic ceremony for baptism has traditionally included a prayer for exorcism, just in case the baby has already picked up some demonic influence from the outside world. I used to thing this exorcism prayer was a harsh and needless part of the beautiful baptismal ceremony. But I have changed my mind, and recognize the wisdom of praying for the child to be freed of any thing evil he may already have picked up from his family or environment[112].

Note that many Christians do not baptize children but instead dedicate the child to the Lord. According to Horrobin, this ceremony would also be an excellent opportunity to exercise authority over any generational spirit inherited from ancestors[113].

Finally, I would like to make a remark on terminology. Some authors use terms like "familiar" or "ancestral" spirits interchangeably with generational spirits as we have described in this book[114]. However, I prefer to avoid these terms since there doesn't seem to be consensus on their definitions. Indeed, some describe familiar spirits as evil spirits that are close to us. They are familiar in the sense of being customary, not familial. We become accustomed to their presence to the point where we start to believe they are good, say these teachers[115]. Others refer to familiar spirits assigned to witches to carry out their malevolent tasks[116]. Finally, some use both terms (familiar or ancestral) to refer

---

112 MacNutt (Francis), *op. cit.* p. 188.
113 Horrobin (Peter J.), *op. cit.*, p. 245.
114 [Online] https://ne np.facebook.com/DemonologieEtRelationDAide/posts/422673197765820/ (January 2021).
115 [Online] https://www.editions-menor.com/fr/livres/34-faire-face-aux-esprits-familiers.html (August 2020).
116 [Online] https://fr.wikipedia.org/wiki/Familier_(esprit) (August 2020).

to human spirits of deceased individuals or demons pretending to be deceased family members[117]. Therefore, I believe it is better to stick to the terminology I suggest. Generational spirits refer to spirits that can be passed down to subsequent generations. They are acquired by ancestors as a result of sins they have committed, traumas they have endured, occult practices they have engaged in, or curses pronounced against them and their descendants.

---

117 MacNutt (Francis), *op.cit.* p. 95. See also :
[Online] https://www.lasaintete.com/etude-biblique-du-mardi-15-mars-2016-invoquer-les-esprits-de-morts-les-esprits-familiers/ (August 2020).
[Online] https://www.gotquestions.org/Francais/esprits-familiers.html (August 2020).

9
The ministry of Jesus

Jesus and the covenants

Now we will examine some episodes from the life of Jesus that allude to various topics discussed in this book. Our first story tells of a woman whom Jesus healed in the midst of a synagogue on the Sabbath day (Lk 13:10-17). The evangelist Luke takes the trouble to tell us that she is a daughter of Abraham. She is a true Israelite, heir to the unconditional covenant promising God's favor to Abraham and his descendants. Yet, she is crippled, bent over for eighteen years. Jesus must have taken the time to speak to her and inquire about her situation, unless he knew it by a supernatural word of knowledge (1 Cor 12:8). Jesus certainly also felt compassion for her, to the point of daring to heal her on a Sabbath day. Indeed, he knew very well that he would provoke the dissatisfaction of legalistic Jews by doing so. As a matter of fact, the synagogue leader reproaches him for performing this miracle on the only day when complete rest was prescribed. Jesus then calls them hypocrites: they all give water to their animals on the Sabbath day, and yet they would refuse this miracle to this poor woman!

But that's not all. Luke, who is a physician, specifies that this woman is infirm because of a demon and that she is bound by Satan. These are not trivial details, especially coming from the mouth of an educated man capable of making medical diagnoses. The text even uses the word *ekho*, which means "to possess." The French Louis Segond 1910 version speaks of a "possessed woman." The Nouvelle Bible Segond avoids commenting on the delicate subject of demonic possession by simply stating that she is "made infirm by a spirit[118]" just as the NIV version does in English. The Darby and the King James versions present to us a "woman having a spirit of infirmity." Whatever the conclusions of the exegesis of this text, whether this woman is "possessed" or she "possesses" the spirit, one thing is certain, according to Luke, she is indeed infirm because of this spirit, and not as a result of a physical illness[119].

How will Jesus act next? He first declares the woman's liberation by speaking with authority: "Woman, you are freed." Then he lays his hands on her, and she is immediately healed. Some think she did not have an evil spirit because elsewhere in the Bible, Jesus does not touch the demon-possessed. But demon-possessed individuals are usually very agitated. Here, this is not the case. Moreover, we observe that Jesus first declared her liberation before touching the woman. Peter Horrobin therefore thinks that the spirit had left before Jesus touched her[120].

This story interests us because a pious Israelite woman, attending the synagogue and heir to the covenants, is nevertheless infirm because of an evil spirit. It is probably not a generational spirit, as it is mentioned that this has been going on for eighteen years, and not since her birth. But this proves that the chosen ones who love God can, despite a favorable covenant, be harassed by demons. Furthermore, it demonstrates that demons also attack the health of the body, not just the mental state of the person. Therefore, this is a solid biblical argument against the belief that mentally ill people were called demon-possessed in Jesus' time. Here, it is clear that Jesus perceived a demon in a person who was physically ill.

---

118 For a discussion on the subject of possession, see my book E*spoir pour l'âme et l'esprit, le miracle de la guérison intérieure.*

119 Luke was probably not present. But he wrote his Gospel and the Acts of the Apostles by conducting rigorous journalistic work (Lk 1:1-2; Acts 1:1).

120 Horrobin (Peter J.), *op. cit.*, p. 189.

Jesus and the root of evil

This second story takes place in a crowded house (Lk 5:17-26). The crowd has come to hear this rabbi preach, who is now attracting the attention of the people because he is healing the sick. Some people brought their paralyzed friend, and to reach Jesus, they have to go through the roof. This act of faith and their perseverance in helping their friend amazes Jesus. But what happens next is rather surprising. He tells this man that his sins are forgiven. Why? Does he perceive that this man's illness was caused by his sins?

Jesus acts, therefore, for this paralyzed man in a completely different way than he did for the paralyzed woman in the previous story. Sometimes, he discerns a demon that he casts out before praying for physical healing. Here, he forgives sins before declaring physical healing. Jesus seems to perceive the root cause of the illness and prays accordingly. These texts support this notion and demonstrate the importance of this step.

Jesus and curses

Nothing reveals Jesus's indignation towards the curses humanity has to endure more than his attitude towards a desperate leper who comes to him and begs to be healed (Mk 1:40-45). This leper does not adhere to the required social distancing due to his condition. He dares to come to Jesus. He is convinced that the Lord can heal him, but he wonders if he wants to. Will he be rejected by him like the rest of humanity? Indeed, lepers were ostracized in Israel. Their suffering was both social and physical because the Law stipulated it.

And the leper in whom the plague is, his clothes shall be rent, and his head bore, and he shall put a covering on his upper lip, and shall cry, Unclean, unclean. All the days wherein the plague shall be in him he shall be defiled; he is unclean: he shall dwell alone; without the camp shall his habitation be.

Leviticus 13:45-46

Leprosy was considered a punishment from God. Everyone in Israel knew the story of Miriam who had challenged the authority of her brother Moses (Num 12:1-15). They also knew that King Uzziah had been struck with leprosy when he became angry because the high priest had specified to him, according to the Law, what he was forbidden to do in offering incense to the Lord (2 Chron 26:17-21). And who hadn't heard of Elisha's servant, Gehazi, who became leprous after demanding a gift from Naaman and lying about it to his master (2 Kgs 5:20-27)?

However, there were indeed many other terrible diseases in Israel at that time. Why does Jesus pay special attention to this one? Is it not because it is linked to sin and social exclusion? Furthermore, the ritual confirming the healing of leprosy strangely resembles the crucifixion of Christ. Indeed, the healed leper had to go to the priest. He would leave the inhabited area (Lev 14:3) as Jesus did when going to Golgotha (Heb 13:11-12). The priest would then slaughter a bird and mix its blood with living water, then dip a second live bird into it (Lev 14:4-7). The blood symbolizes the redemption of the sinner and the living water the Holy Spirit (Jn 4:10-11; 7:38-39; 1 Jn 5:6-8). Note that water and blood also flowed from Jesus' pierced side (Jn 19:34-35). Finally, according to the evangelist preacher Benny Hinn, in this ceremony, there was also cedarwood representing the cross, scarlet to symbolize suffering, and hyssop to represent faith[121].

The healing of leprosy also represents the end of social rejection. Indeed, the purification of lepers allowed them to reintegrate into the community. This healing is therefore a sign pointing to the ability of the kingdom of God to intervene with the disadvantaged, the poor, and the rejected, in order to break the curses that affect them and unite them with a welcoming community.

Jesus cares deeply about healing leprosy out of compassion, but also for the sign it represents. That's why when he sends his disciples on a mission, he takes the trouble to tell them, "Cleanse

---

121 Hinn (Benny), *Le sang de l'alliance,* Nîmes, Vida, 1999, p. 68.

the lepers" and "heal the sick" (Mt 10:8). Moreover, when the disciples of John the Baptist question him to know if he is truly the Messiah, he then says, "The blind receive sight, the lame walk, those who have leprosy are cleansed, the deaf hear, the dead are raised, and the good news is proclaimed to the poor" (Mt 11:5). His response indicates that the healing of leprosy is one of the messianic signs. Leprosy is therefore not just any disease. It represents the social action of the Church.

Jesus therefore warmly welcomes our leper (Mk 1:41). The text says that the Lord is moved in His emotions (*splanchnisthesis*). Note that some Greek texts instead have the term *orgisthesis*[122], which means "indignation" or "anger," which supports our argument about social justice. If we combine these two ancient versions of the text, Jesus would have felt a mixture of frustration and sadness towards the condition of this man.

These verbs also remind us of Jesus's reaction at the tomb of his friend Lazarus. In this other episode of Jesus's life, he "groaned in the spirit, and was troubled" (Jn 11:33). Here, the term "groaned" is *enebrimesato*; it expresses anger. The second verb, *etaraxen,* denotes agitation, confusion, and disorganization[123]. Jesus's emotion is not simply sadness at losing a friend. The Lord is revolted by death and by all the curses that humanity must endure because of sin. This indignation towards evil is a characteristic of God. Without a doubt, Jesus hated to see evil invade the world He had created.

Another important detail, Jesus decides to touch this leper. He could have acted differently, as the Bible reports that he was

---

122 Some commentators try to relate the Greek term e*mbrimaomai* in Mark 1:43, which indicates that Jesus spoke "sternly" to the leper. But this latter attitude is explained. Jesus wanted to prevent the man from telling his story to everyone, which could complicate his movements afterward. Wessel (Wlater W.), *The Expositor's Bible Commentary, op. cit.* Text and endnotes.
123 Merril (Tenney C.), *The Expositor's Bible Commentary.*

capable of healing from a distance (Mt 8:5-13). Normally, one does not touch a leper to avoid catching their disease and to obey the Law that forbids touching what is unclean. But Jesus teaches that impurity is a state of the heart and not of the body (Mt 15:18-20). It also seems that the absolute purity of the Lord protected him from disease. This gesture is deliberate and significant. When the leper feels Jesus's hand, hope rises in him: "Here is a man who does not reject me, and who even dares to touch me. He is surely stronger than my disease. This Jesus can and wants to heal me! And he loves me enough to welcome me, and even to defy the Law to save me."

It is not easy to imitate Jesus in this regard. Paul Olson, an American missionary, visited a leper village in West Africa. New Hope[124], he says, is a village filled with outcast lepers who have come from everywhere. Their bodies are mutilated by the disease, but they thirst for the Gospel. It is written on all the walls: "Do not touch the lepers." However, what moved our missionary the most happened when these very special sick people gathered in front of the stage where he was to speak, and began to sing:

> Ha do, dear friend from across the briny deep.
> Thank you for coming so far to tell us the story of Jesus.
> We would like to shake your hand to welcome you proper,
> but we cannot, you see, for we are lepers.
> So we wave our hands to you and say ha do[125].

On the stage, Olson could only cry. A strange emotion had overwhelmed him, a mix of compassion, indignation, and anger. As he left the village, he also felt shame because he had not dared to touch the lepers. I am not saying that we must touch them, but it is clear to see the greatness of the Son of God, who did not hesitate to cross one of the greatest social barriers to free us. God does not

---

124 [Online] http://fiohnetwork.org/ ?p=1620 (Novembre 2020).
125 Olson (Paul), *How to Touch a Leper*, Mound [MN], New Day Publishing Company, 1986, pp. 55-56.

only want us to announce the forgiveness of sins or to heal the sick; He also desires to break the isolation, rejection, and curses experienced by those who suffer. The human condition that stems from original sin touches His heart. He wants to deliver us from all the consequences of Adam and Eve's fall, which have been passed down from generation to generation and affect society in various ways.

Jesus and demonized children

Two biblical accounts report the deliverance of demon-possessed children. The first is an epileptic boy (Mk 9:17-29). The description of his seizure resembles a generalized convulsion of the "grand mal" type. The father says he has a "mute" spirit. Jesus does not contradict him. In praying to cast it out, he even specifies that it is a "deaf and mute" spirit. How did Jesus know this detail: through supernatural knowledge or by discussing with the father? The text does not say. However, we know that Jesus asked at least one question to the father: "How long has this been happening to him?" Why this question? Jesus is likely trying to understand the entry point of the demon. The father responds that it has been happening since he was a very small child. He does not report any particular event. When the story is not more precise, we can suspect a generational spirit. Randy Clark says he often sees generational spirits and that he has already seen demon-possessed babies. Horrobin reports cases of generational spirits linked to satanic practices involving sacrificing children by first gouging out their eyes and ears and cutting out their tongues. He explains that demons then enter the baby, and when it dies, they infest those who attended the ceremony. Such demons can then cause deafness, muteness, or blindness, depending on the tortures practiced. These demons are then generally passed down to the descendants of these satanists. It is therefore not impossible that the ancestors of this epileptic, deaf, and mute child were worshippers of Canaanite gods and practiced such horrors. It should not be concluded, obviously, that all epileptics, or all deaf and mute people are demon-possessed. This is why Jesus may have wanted to clarify the diagnosis and the entry point.

Jesus also helped another young girl possessed by demons. In fact, he did not even see this child (Mk 7:24-30). Her mother came to beg Jesus to heal her. This young girl was probably too tormented to be brought to Jesus. The emphasis here is on the fact that Jesus was in foreign territory. This mother, of Syrophoenician origin, was not a daughter of Abraham. She was initially refused deliverance by Jesus. However, Jesus never refused to heal the sick in Israel. How can this refusal be explained? The outpouring of the Spirit had not yet taken place. The kingdom of heaven was not yet accessible to the Gentiles. In contrast, the Israelites were under the protection of divine covenants, of which Jesus was the fulfillment and fullness. Moreover, he was conducting a ministry among Israel to demonstrate that he was the awaited Messiah. Additionally, we see that Jesus spoke a parable indicating that when we cast out a demon, we must protect the delivered person by praying that they be filled with the Spirit of God—or at least ensure they are protected by an unconditional covenant (Mt 12:43-45).

The story, however, has an unexpected outcome, which explains why this account is found in the Holy Scriptures. This woman expresses to Jesus that she recognizes him as her master and asks only for the crumbs that fall from his table. Jesus acknowledges that this woman's faith is remarkable. He then declares the child healed by proxy, based on the mother's declaration. Indeed, the child is under the cover and authority of the parent. This principle is important when we pray for generational bonds: when we free an adult, we can also pray to deliver their minor children.

Another observation can be drawn from this passage. Jesus says that he cannot give the children's bread of Israel to the little dogs. The term "dogs" here refers to non-Jews. The metaphor is not pejorative. It emphasizes that the most common food, bread, which is eaten every day, is for humans and not for domestic animals. This means that deliverance is part of the regular and normal practices within the circle of those who are in the family of God. The same logic extrapolated today would mean that deliverance is a legitimate and expected privilege on a regular basis, normally reserved for Christians. Therefore, a Christian can be demonized, but can also be delivered. And a non-Christian filled with faith, like this woman, can exceptionally be liberated.

Additionally, note that in both accounts, prayer plays an important role. The foreign woman begs Jesus and insists that he heal her daughter. Her perseverance is rewarded. In the case of the young boy, the disciples could not heal him, and Jesus explains that this type of demon only comes out through prayer and fasting. This indicates that some deliverance sessions are more difficult than others. There are situations where we must prepare ourselves in prayer and plead our case before God. Sometimes, we do not understand what prevents deliverance from occurring. Personally, I witnessed a woman for whom we prayed, but she was not immediately delivered. Several elements of her story led us to believe that members of her extended family had sought to prosper by using her family as an offering through witchcraft practices. She therefore had to engage in a long battle to be delivered from physical and psychological attacks[126].

Jesus and generational sins

In this last episode that we recount, it is said that the illness of our subject dates back to his birth (Jn 9:1-41). Jesus' disciples ask a question that interests us: "Who sinned, this man or his

---

[126] Horrobin mentions that it is sometimes better for deliverance not to occur in a single session because it would be too overwhelming; however, this does not mean that one should have to pray for years, as in this case. *Ibid,* p. 186.

parents, that he was born blind?" These men see this illness as a curse and want to know if the blind man is responsible for his own misfortune or if he is the victim of his ancestors' sins. Both could cause such an infirmity, and a gift of discernment is needed to know the cause. Essentially, the disciples are asking, "What do you discern, Jesus?"

A modern reader might find the idea that the blind man could have committed a sin before his birth strange. However, it seems that the idea that an embryo could sin was indeed widespread among the rabbis of Jesus' time[127]! The transmission of the fathers' iniquity was also recognized. Furthermore, we see later that the scribes tell the healed blind man that he was "born entirely in sin" (v. 34). Additionally, they refuse to acknowledge this healing because, to heal such a man, one would need the power to annul the fault of the fetus or the sin of the ancestors. However, only God could forgive sins (Mk 2:7) and annul their consequences. Hence, the incredulity of the authorities: "How could a man who is a sinner perform such miraculous signs?" (v. 16).

I do not know of any theologian today who defends the idea that an embryo can commit a sin. However, Jesus does not tell the disciples that their question is foolish, which suggests that this concept was as recognized as that of generational iniquities. Instead, Jesus responds by saying that neither this man nor his parents sinned. In this blind man's case, the entry point was not a personal or familial sin. Our illnesses sometimes stem simply from our general condition as sinners, that is, from original sin. This man might have had a genetic disease, or he could have contracted an infection during pregnancy, such as toxoplasmosis or rubella[128].

---

127 Merril (Tenney C.), *The healing of the blind man* (John 9:1-41), *The Expositor's Bible Commentary*.
128 All diseases stem from the deterioration of creation as a result of original sin.

Then Jesus tells the disciples that this situation is a good opportunity to act and teach a great truth. Once healed, this blind man gradually understands who it is that restored his sight: a righteous man, a prophet; and not just any prophet! Could he be the Messiah? He ponders this while discussing with the religious leaders who inquire about his condition. Eventually, the miracle recipient finds Jesus again, who reveals himself to him as the Son of God. And the whole question of spiritual blindness is then raised. The one who was blind can now see. Those who claim to see are actually blind because they do not recognize their Messiah: the sinless Man-God who has the power to forgive, to heal, and to rise on the third day, according to the Scriptures. Jesus' purpose is fulfilled. The work of God is manifested, and the truth proclaimed: Jesus is the light of the world (v. 5).

All these accounts are reassuring. Because, no matter the cause of our sufferings, the Son of God can always heal us. Jesus desires to alleviate humanity and make himself known as the Savior. All the stories of his life show that he is a man of action and reacts from the depths of his being upon seeing the curses afflicting humanity. He came to set the captives free (Lk 4:18). He is still with us today to help us discern the entry points of our infirmities and then bring us healing.

10
The practice of liberation

We will now conclude this overview by addressing the practical aspects of breaking generational ties. However, a preliminary remark is necessary before we begin. It's important to recognize that generational issues are never isolated. Prayers for generational ties are only one part of the interventions made within the broader framework of inner healing prayer. Ideally, we should pray for both the personal and generational aspects of our wounds, sins, and oppressions. To be healed comprehensively, those seeking help must also release their personal sufferings, forgive those who have wronged them, confess their own faults, and renounce what they themselves have practiced in the occult world. Some spirits that do not have a generational origin are then expelled. Just as a boat cannot leave the dock until all moorings are removed, similarly, unless one receives the grace of instant healing, people are healed when we have addressed all aspects of their problems[129].

Before we begin to pray, we must determine who will be part of our team. In inner healing prayer, we emphasize healing as much, if not more, than deliverance. In this case, a team of two helpers is appropriate. When praying to break generational ties, this duo will be sufficient in most cases. However, if we know from the outset that the person we are assisting is harassed by demons or that there has been witchcraft in the family, we prefer to form a larger team. We will then ask individuals with particularly effective discernment of spirits to join us. We will determine in advance who will be the initial leader of the group and who can relay them.

---

[129] To better understand how to pray for the personal aspects bringing healing, I encourage you to refer to my *Manuel de formation*.

It is also important that the helpers are in good standing with God. Of course, no one is perfect! However, we must confess our sins before God before we begin. We must also be in good relationship with the other team members. We proclaim peace upon the place where we are. We place ourselves under God's protection and ask for His favor to discern what He wants us to do in His name.

When we pray, it is important to enter into the presence of God and ask for the direction of His Spirit. The place where we are should be filled with reverence, worship, and praise towards God. Furthermore, we affirm our faith in Christ and our desire to be united and consecrated to Him alone. The fruit of the Spirit flows from this attitude and such an atmosphere. Peace, joy, love, faith, and hope are present. All our prayers will then be based on the work of Jesus Christ on the cross. It is very important to understand that propitiation contains everything needed to bind the power of the enemy. Jesus reigns: "God has highly exalted him, and given him a name which is above every name: that at the name of Jesus every knee should bow, of things in heaven, and things in earth, and things under the earth" (Phil 2:9-10). The Son of God has all authority in heaven and on earth (Mt 28:18). Through Jesus Christ who came in the flesh, everything is accessible, but not automatic upon conversion. We will need to ask and exercise our authority.

We have authority in Jesus to overcome the enemy. But we must also avoid triumphalism and arrogance. *Yet Michael the archangel, when contending with the devil he disputed about the body of Moses, dared not bring against him a railing accusation, but said, The Lord rebuke you* (Jude 9). We must recognize our limitations and exercise this ministry according to the measure of faith the Lord has given us (Rom 12:3). Sometimes, we may need to end a session in order to direct the one being helped to someone with more authority over certain demons or more discernment than us. This kind of situation can occur, for example, when ancestors have gone far in the practice of witchcraft. In this case, we bind the spirits and proclaim peace over the one being helped until we can definitively cast them out. In the majority of cases, however, generational ties can be easily broken. So, let us approach this ministry with a humble and confident attitude, knowing that it is Jesus who delivers, and we are companions equipped with a clear mandate.

> *Behold, I give to you power*
> *to tread on serpents and scorpions,*
> *and over all the power of the enemy:*
> *and nothing shall by any means hurt you.*
> Luke 10:19

Regardless of the immediate goal of the encounter, we keep in mind that the ministry of deliverance works hand in hand with the ministry of inner healing. We work with the person being helped in an attitude of love and honor. Our goal is to take care of this person even when demons manifest. And all this beautiful work is also part of the sanctification of the Christian. Indeed, inner healing prayer follows the same thought as the theology of sanctification. When we believe that Christ died for our sins, we are reconciled with God and justified. At that moment, God cancels all condemnation and gives us eternal life (Rom 8:1, 29-30). We then enter into a process of transformation whereby the Holy Spirit instructs and energizes us so that we have the will and ability to resemble Jesus more closely, as we are now part of God's people (2 Cor 7:1; Phil 2:13; 3:13-14; Col 1:28).

The word "holiness" translates the Hebrew word *qadesh* and the Greek word *hagios*. These terms mean "separation" or "splendor." The idea is to be set apart from the world and dedicated to God to reflect His glory. This consecration involves a transformation of thinking and acting, a renewal of the image of God that has been altered by original sin (Rom 12:1-2; Eph 4:20-24). The apostle Paul uses the term "sanctified" to refer to the initial setting apart, the call to be a child of God from conversion (1 Cor 1:2; 6:11). But

Paul and other biblical authors also describe a quest, a struggle that is part of a long-term process.

> *You have not yet resisted to blood, striving against sin.*
> *Follow peace with all men, and holiness,*
> *without which no man shall see the Lord.*
>
> Hebrew 12:4,14

The apostles teach that sanctification is more than acquiring moral character through personal effort to adhere to the standards of the Christian community. It is a circumcision of the heart, a spiritual renewal performed by the Spirit of God (Rom 2:29). This process is filled with obstacles, successes, and setbacks. We will walk in it until the final victory when Christ returns, for Jesus did not come only for us to decide to believe that He died for our sins. He wants Christians to grow and be delivered from all evil (Lk 4:18-19).

To achieve this goal of comprehensive liberation, there must be repentance, which means a willingness to turn to God and change. Additionally, the believer must live in union with Christ. It is then that they will find healing of the heart and liberation of the spirit. However, this does not happen without actively cooperating with God. Indeed, when a person has been wounded, it is very common for them to commit sins in reaction to their wounds. Sometimes, these take the form of chronic behaviors that become ingrained in the person's life; for example, rebellion, independence, criticism. We are responsible for these sins, and every sin must be confessed. But if we want these reactive behaviors to stop, we must embark on a healing journey that involves surrendering our pains to Christ, forgiving those who have wronged us, and then renouncing our sins. This healing process is a journey towards holiness.

Teachers who claim that Christians do not need inner healing for their wounds, asserting that everything is accomplished at the moment of conversion, often rely on 2 Corinthians 5:17 to argue that old things have passed away and the new convert is a new creature. However, we are not automatically freed from our wounds by becoming Christians. To claim otherwise is to deny an evident reality! That's why several scholars translate the Greek word *ktisis* in 2 Corinthians 5:17 as "creation" rather than "creature," as the latter sense is also possible. Thus, conversion sets us apart and brings us into a new creation. We then embark on a transformation process in which we put to death the old man and allow Christ to live in us (Gal 2:20; Col 1:27).

Interestingly, among these teachers who challenge healing approaches, many do not have the same attitude regarding sins. There, one would need to work hard to strengthen their character! This reasoning is not consistent. If being a new creature eliminates our wounds, then why not also our vices? Moreover, this moralizing view of sin contradicts its deep nature. It denies the dynamic relationship between our wounds and our sins. There is no reason to separate the various aspects of salvation: on one side sins, and on the other healing and deliverance. For example, the apostles used the Greek word *sozo* as much in the sense of "saving" as in "healing."

Furthermore, I have noticed that these same pastors who argue that we do not need inner healing or deliverance have often witnessed the damage caused by modern psychology in the lives of believers. They want to protect the people of God from unhealthy introspection and the influence of atheistic humanistic thought. On this point, I agree with them. Introspection can be a destructive habit for their flock if it only aims to seek causes for their problems or to wallow in self-pity. The protective intention of these pastors is commendable, but denying wounds is not the solution to advocate for.

Historically, Christianity has always advocated for self-examination leading to confession, as we do in our ministry of inner healing. This approach is quite different from the victimization perpetuated by some introspective methods. These pastors' reaction does not consider that Christianity can intervene through biblical prayers that will be effective. Moreover, inner healing prayer contributes to sanctifying the individuals who require this type of assistance. This relatively brief intervention brings about significant transformations in the thinking and behavior of those helped. By discovering this type of assistance, they also learn that they can approach God at any time to lay down their suffering and forgive those who have offended them.

Prayers aimed at breaking generational curses are part of the healing and sanctification process that relies on Christ's propitiation. The pursuit of holiness is precisely the context of 1 Pet 1:18, a text often cited in relation to the negative legacies received from our ancestors.

> *[...] but like the Holy One who called you,*
> *be holy yourselves also in all your behavior;*
> *because it is written,*
> *"YOU SHALL BE HOLY, FOR I AM HOLY."*
> *If you address as Father the One who impartially judges*
> *according to each one's work,*
> *conduct yourselves in fear*
> *during the time of your stay on earth;*
> *knowing that you were not redeemed*
> *with perishable things like silver or gold*
> *from your futile way of life inherited from your forefathers,*
> *but with precious blood, as of a lamb unblemished and spotless,*
> *the blood of Christ.*
>
> 1 Peter 1:15-19 (NAS)

There is indeed a connection here between the pursuit of holiness, the liberation from negative generational legacies, and the power of Christ's propitiation. However, we must be cautious when citing 1 Peter 1:18 as evidence of the existence of generational ties and not read more into this text than it actually tells us. It concerns the inheritance of a sinful lifestyle. Peter does not necessarily refer here to oppressive ties. Furthermore, the mode of transmission is not specified by Peter. This way of life could be passed down through upbringing or genetics, just as it may involve spiritual generational ties. Therefore, let us primarily focus on the entirety of the passage. God desires our holiness. It is obtained through regeneration in Christ, who can free us from any negative inheritance from our ancestors.

Checking the basics

When we receive a person for inner healing prayer, our approach begins by checking certain things with the person being helped. First, have they been born again? If not, and if we have ties to break or spirits to cast out, we need to explain that these ties often return to people who are not inhabited by the Holy Spirit. This is why we prefer to wait until the person being helped is able to respond positively to the message of the Gospel before starting a process of liberation that goes beyond the healing of the soul[130].

If the person being helped is a believer, we still ask if they believe in the existence of demons and their activity among Christians. Are they ready to open their heart? To fight in prayer? To change their lifestyle, if necessary, in order to follow Jesus as a true disciple? A negative answer to any of these questions should postpone any intervention until the person is better disposed, as a lack of obedience allows the enemy to resist.

I usually do not ask these questions immediately to those I help. The fact of obtaining their written consent during an official request for inner healing shows me that they are ready to collaborate, that

---

130 However, we sometimes see demons manifesting in an evangelization context. It is possible and even desirable to practice deliverance in this context, while explaining to the person being helped the necessity for them to choose life in Christ (Acts 5:16; 8:7). Helpers sometimes also decide to pray for non-believers when it is a matter of life or death; for example, when a person hears voices telling them to kill themselves.

they are not acting because of pressure from their surroundings or in the heat of the moment. However, I question them if their reactions make me suspect a lack of determination. On the other hand, if you do not require an official written request, it would be appropriate to assess the motivation of the person you are helping during the first interview.

Reconstructing history

Our approach must include gathering information on the personal and family history. We can collect this data by asking questions or by reconstructing the history from a less guided conversation. We prefer the latter option. Initially, we pray to ask Jesus to guide us by communicating the relevant things to us. We remain silent and listen. Then the person being helped tells us what they perceived: an image, a word, a memory, etc. We then discuss the meaning of this revelation and what it evokes in them. We generally listen more than once, asking increasingly specific questions to the Lord. This usually leads to a significant memory. We formulate our prayers when we have enough elements in hand.

It is very rare for the topic of parents not to be addressed. In doing so, we can generally get a good idea of the family history. We suspect ancestral ties when the Lord shows us, or when the person being helped reports repetitive patterns from one generation to another. Sometimes, the person seeking help will have observed these patterns themselves; other times, it is the helpers who note them. The absence of a personal history explaining a compulsive attitude is also a criterion leading us to investigate the presence of generational ties. If we suspect such ties, we pray to learn more and to trace back to the origin of these ties. We rely on a word of knowledge to reveal the sins and wounds of their ancestors, as it is not easy to know the distant events that gave the enemy access. Most of us only know our family for two generations. We are unaware of the lives and, even more so, the sins committed several generations ago. Another possibility would be to do research and create a family tree, but we do not use this method. Finally, we can use a list that enumerates occult practices. By reading this list while praying, it is possible that a particular element catches the attention of the person being helped, and the Spirit indicates that their ancestors were part of a certain sect or used a certain occult method in the past. Sometimes, a word will rekindle the memory of clues they observed in the family. Despite all these tools, the revelation we receive about entry points is often only partial. We pray based on what we have and rely on God's grace.

Once the basics are checked and historical markers are established to look for entry points, we are now ready to break the generational ties by praying with the aim to:
1. Confess and cover iniquity;
2. Cancel curses;
3. Break generational ties;
4. Renounce alliances;
5. Cast out spirits.

Confessing and covering iniquity

The first aspect of the prayer to counter generational ties is to confess and cover the iniquity of the ancestors to close the doors to the enemy. We have explained that propitiation is the act by which God covers sins. When we ask God for this, the blood of Jesus that sealed the New Covenant covers our sins and those of our ancestors in His eyes. Everything is accomplished by His perfect sacrifice. However, we must appeal to what Christ has done for us. The person being helped can, as a representative of the family, mention the sins committed by their ancestors and confess them. The idea here is not to ask God to forgive the ancestors. We cannot annul their actions. God will judge each person's deeds as He sees fit (Heb 9:27). However, we can ask

God to cover the sins of the ancestors so that they no longer have consequences for their descendants. We can also forgive our ancestors for the consequences their sins have had on us. In short, we confess their sins to cover them, not to obtain their salvation, and we forgive them.

When the generational tie has been caused by trauma, it is important to forgive those who hurt our ancestors. Again, these acts of forgiveness do not absolve the aggressors. By forgiving, we leave judgment to God and release any anger and bitterness we might have against them. For example, a woman with a deficient mother, who herself was raised by a grandmother abused by a neighbor, could forgive that neighbor, her grandmother, and her mother. Indeed, besides the actions committed by the mother herself, the abuse committed by a stranger would have affected the entire family dynamic.

Sometimes, a person being helped does not understand my explanations and asks God to forgive their ancestors or asks for forgiveness from God on behalf of their ancestors. In these situations, I gently interrupt and re-explain that they can only forgive their ancestors for the consequences this has had on them. They can also confess their ancestors' sins to ask God to cover them to cancel the curses; but they cannot ask God to annul their ancestors' guilt. Here again, we see how important it is to distinguish between guilt and the consequences of sins.

The helper can assist the person being helped in formulating their prayers if they have difficulty understanding how to pray. The helper can articulate the prayer, and the person being helped repeats it. The helper then acts as a priest, standing between the person being helped and God to intercede, as every believer can do in the New Covenant (1 Pet 2:9; Rev 5:10).

In response to our prayers, God covers the ancestors' sins to render them ineffective. Thus, He cancels the consequences of past wrong actions and wounds for the current generation. This confession reminds God of His covenant :

> *If they shall confess their iniquity,*
> *and the iniquity of their fathers, [...]*
> *Then will I remember my covenant with Jacob,*
> *and also my covenant with Isaac,*
> *and also my covenant with Abraham will I remember;*
> *and I will remember the land.*
>
> Leviticus 26:40,42

Undo curses

We generally add to the prayers aimed at covering sins, words to break curses and the atmosphere bequeathed to the present generation, regardless of the source of these curses (sins or traumas of the ancestors, self-curses, or curses against the family).

For example, when praying for the child of a teenage mother who was a victim of fornication, we can ask that the child not be affected by the consequences related to the situation[131]. Similarly, when praying against a curse pronounced by an ancestor who declared that he and his descendants are all born to a small destiny (poverty mentality), we would declare that the spoken word is broken and that the curse no longer applies to the family.

Regarding curses coming from outside the family through acts of witchcraft, we will take the time to enumerate the practices that may have been done, in order to break them one by one. We will declare ineffective the rites, sacrifices, words, exchanges of money, etc. We will annul the mandates of these dark acts. It is very useful here to have the gift of discernment to perceive exactly what has been done and the effect of our prayers. If we do not have this gift, it is very important to follow up with the

---

131 These issues were described in chapter 7.

person and refer them to a more experienced helper if our prayers do not achieve the desired result.

Break generational ties

The negative generational ties must then be severed by our prayers, separating the person being helped from their ancestors. We aim to free individuals who feel compelled to repeat certain sins or who unwittingly reproduce the traumatic patterns of their ancestors. We also separate individuals whose identity is still merged with another person. This prayer breaks these ties in a specific area, for example: a son who is violent or commits incest like his father and grandfather; a daughter who replicates hatred towards men or undergoes abortion like her mother and grandmother; a woman still merged with her mother or associated with her sick aunt.

Taking the example we discussed earlier, of the daughter of a teenage mother, we know from research that she is 7.5 times more likely than other girls her age to follow in her mother's footsteps. Therefore, we can immediately pray to break this tie. If the pattern has already repeated, we can pray for the young child of this mother to be released from this fate if it is a daughter. Indeed, we believe that minor children of those we help can be liberated in response to our prayers, as they are under the authority of the parent. However, adult children should make their own journey. For safety measures, Horrobin recommends that someone be with the minor child when they are not present where we pray. However, just like us, he has never seen reactions from these children during such prayers[132].

The way to pray to sever a generational tie is simply to declare that the tie is broken based on the work of Jesus Christ. Additionally, we often instruct those we help to visualize the tie

---

132 Horrobin (Peter J.), *op. cit.*, p. 182.

(a rope, chain, etc.), and then imagine a tool of their choice to cut it (scissors, axe, chainsaw). This mental imagery enhances the volitional capacity and also allows us to see in the spirit whether the tie breaks or resists our prayers. Mrs. Payne describes the effects of this approach here.

> As the Holy Spirit controls the situation and the healing process is powerfully at work, the patient always has a revealing image of her mother, which allows her, for the first time, to see her mother objectively, encouraging her to forgive her completely. Then, I ask her to see if there is any remaining tie between her and her mother. If so, she sees it and names it, and I tell her, as if she had scissors in her hand, to cut these ties she sees. The liberation that follows is often almost phenomenal; sometimes the women I pray for also experience quite strong emotional or physical reactions. One woman may see these ties as a frayed umbilical cord, another as ropes connecting the two souls, etc. When these ties are severed, we see an image that has symbolic value but represents the reality of the deliverance and separation that has occurred[133].

Finally, we also pray to confess the personal sins of the person being helped in the areas where they are bound. They are always responsible for their actions even if they have reproduced the pattern of their ancestors by inheriting a generational tie. Indeed, a person bound by such a tie can never claim "it's not my fault." This tendency to sin should be fought against, just like the consequences of original sin.

Renounce alliances

In certain situations, our prayer must include renouncing consents that were granted by ancestors. The difference between a tie and an alliance is the voluntary aspect of the alliance, while a tie

---

[133] Payne (Leanne), *Crise de la masculinité, op. cit.*, pp. 126-127. Translated back to English.

can affect us passively. A testament or any other vow pronounced by an ancestor expressing their will for their descendants are examples of such alliances. In the spiritual realm, the most common situation is occultism because it creates an alliance with the world of darkness, which always has consequences for descendants. Some groups, such as the Freemasons, specifically target the descendants of their followers. By renouncing the alliance created by ancestors and breaking the vows made, descendants dissociate themselves from the clauses of the alliance.

We do not recite pre-prepared prayers, although we know models that generally serve as a guide. Likewise, it is not enough to say "in the name of Jesus" like the seven sons of Sceva, but to be known by the Lord and to be aware that we have the authority to represent Him (Acts 19:13-17). This is also the reason why we avoid timid prayers. For example, we often correct those we help when they pray by saying, "I would like to renounce..." or "I want to renounce..." We tell them that they should instead take action by saying, "I renounce..."

The complexity of the prayer will vary depending on the elements found in the history or revelations from the Holy Spirit. For example, the person being helped will renounce the alliance that their ancestors entered into with the world of darkness through idolatrous and occult practices. Additionally, they will renounce these practices themselves. We will break any pact sealed in blood. We will nullify the words, rites, and consecration of any child in the ancestral lineage of the person being helped. If there has been Satanism in the family, the person being helped will renounce any inheritance of powers that may have been passed down to them, and they will confess any emotional, physical, or sexual abuse practiced on innocent victims, as well as any blasphemy or sacrilege uttered during these occult rituals or black masses.

When there has been witchcraft among the ancestors, the person being helped sometimes struggles to pronounce these prayers without our help. They feel opposition. Sometimes, their thoughts become muddled, and they can no longer pray. It even happens that we have to drive out these blocking spirits that seek to protect the alliances and confuse the revelations we receive as well as the prayers we make. Additionally, we often proceed by asking the person being helped to repeat after us. I speak slowly and pause after each phrase. I explain the words I use to enable them to understand what they have just said and to internalize it. I maintain eye contact with them and ensure that their attention is focused on what we are doing. Once the prayers of renunciation of alliances are completed, the person being helped often feels a great sense of relief.

Drive out spirits

The person being helped may also have inherited evil spirits from their ancestors. The steps we have previously taken will often have already closed all doors and allowed us to suspect the presence or absence of a demon. However, as a safety measure, if spirits need to be cast out, we will ask the Lord one last time to show us any open doors that we may not have seen so far. We believe, like Leanne Payne and Peter Horrobin, that demons cannot resist when they have nothing left to cling to. Therefore, we proclaim the victory of the Lord and believe that demons must obey. However, if all entry points have not been closed first, physical manifestations more or less spectacular related to the resistance of the demon(s) may occur.

Some authors do not share the view that spirits can be gently cast out following adequate preparation. Derek Prince and Frank and Ida May Hammond, for example, teach that there can be no deliverance without a physical manifestation of the demon's rejection (coughing, spitting, vomiting). Therefore, they encourage the person being helped to make physical efforts to expel the evil spirits. We avoid giving these instructions in advance so as not to suggest anything to the person being helped. However, we encourage them to exhale or cough if they have a spontaneous expulsion reaction and cannot free themselves from the demon. The closure of the doors and the absence of suggestion, in my opinion, explain why we observe few physical reactions[134]. If, despite all our precautions, ugly and impressive physical reactions occur, we then command the demon to calm down and be silent. Then, we try to establish contact with the person. Our goal is to collaborate with the person being helped to find the cause of the resistance.

Similarly, opinions are divided when manifestations occur in a Christian publicly during prayer, praise, or preaching. Some believe that the spirits should be cast out immediately. Others, like me, prefer to bind the demons and calm them, then postpone the deliverance session to later with the aim to first be able to close all entry points. Indeed, I believe that this allows for taking care of the person in a more intimate setting after providing them with adequate explanations. It is distressing to see on the Internet people tormented by demons writhing while surrounded by several Christians all shouting together to cast out spirits. The most distressing thing is that the intensity of the physical reactions observed then does not necessarily mean that the demons will leave the person, that there are more demons than in other cases, or that they are stronger. All we can conclude is that there is at least one demon that we are causing to react and who bullies this person!

To cast out a spirit, we proceed in three steps. The first two resemble what we have done before regarding a generational link, but it is not the same thing here. In this case, our prayer targets the influence of a spirit, not a link. Therefore, we need to:

---

[134] Howerver, we mainly deal with relatively mild cases. Heavier cases of witchcraft can pose more resistance.

1. Renounce: The person renounces the influence of the spirit that feeds their thoughts and accentuates a mindset or behavior; they renounce any advantages, such as a talent, an ability to charm people, or supernatural power, conferred by a demon.
2. Break: The person breaks the influence and grip that this spirit has on them and around them.
3. Cast out: The person asserts belonging to Christ and casts out the spirit by reminding it that it has no right to remain there.

Generally, the helper speaks the words and asks the person being helped to repeat them. However, there is no problem if the person being helped is more active. Finally, it is important to explain to the person being helped that we are not praying to God but addressing the evil spirit directly. We speak to it with authority in the name of Jesus.

We can also invoke the blood of the New Covenant or ask for a powerful intervention of the Spirit. Additionally, like Mrs. Payne, we sometimes use anointing oil or sanctified water[135]. We also have a small wooden cross[136] that we place in the hands of the person being helped, as a last resort, asking them to focus on it and meditate on the work of Jesus. I have never encountered a demon that has resisted this.

---

135 Sanctified water is a solution of water and salt prepared following a liturgical prayer that invokes the power of the Lord. Leanne Payne asserts that demons flee as soon as the person being helped comes into contact with the water. She particularly recommends this method for freeing children by sprinkling their beds, without even informing them of the procedure. We also use it to purify certain places such as a new home. As for oil, it is preferred if there is a physical illness. However, sanctified oil or water do not have inherent power. They act as a symbolic representation of the purification obtained through Jesus, based on the faith placed in him. Payne (Leanne), *Restoring the Christian Soul through healing prayer, op. cit.*, pp. 163-178.

136 Leanne Payne also emphasizes the use of the cross. *Ibid,* pp.179-181.

Finally, it's important to take seriously the possibility that the enemy may attack the helpers following our intervention. Although we know that God is stronger, we must be aware that we are engaged in spiritual warfare. However, we can protect ourselves with a very simple four-point prayer that we recite at the end of the session to cover:

1. The lives of the helpers as well as the person being helped;
2. The lives of our loved ones (family, etc.);
3. Our possessions[137];
4. The possessions of our loved ones[138].

Maintain liberation

As good soldiers, we must secure the ground after every victory over the enemy. Therefore, we pray for the recipient to be filled with the Spirit. Paul also recommends this to every Christian (Eph 5:18). But this is especially true after deliverance because being harassed by demons may have weakened the recipient's spiritual life. The fullness of the Spirit is surely the best guarantee against the return of evil spirits and the patterns attached to traumas and sins. However, we inform the recipient that there may be counterattacks. Even if the demons have been cast out, they may still tempt or accuse them in order to reopen the doors giving them access. Nevertheless, we have observed that this type of harassment does not last long if the recipient knows how to resist and assert authority a few times. Therefore, the initial period is crucial.

To strengthen our recipient, several other suggestions are made to them. Firstly, we encourage them to acknowledge Jesus as the

---

137 I added this request after noticing that there were often breakdowns in the house and on our computers when we went to give conferences that allowed a significant advancement of the kingdom of God.

138 I added this element to my list when my son had an accident while moving. His life and that of my grandson were spared, but their belongings were lost.

Lord of their life, that is, to dedicate themselves entirely to Him in all areas, to develop good devotional habits, and to obey His Word and the Holy Spirit when He speaks. We also recommend that they be baptized in water if they have not already done so and to regularly take communion. We also plead for the recipient to be convinced of the Lord's love for them, which will promote a stronger relationship with Him (Eph 3:14-19).

Secondly, we advise them to maintain good habits in personal hygiene. A healthy diet, restful sleep, and regular exercise are all measures that help a person recover from a dark period or simply maintain good health. Thirdly, we recommend that they join a group of Christians that will stimulate their growth. If needed, we help them locate one and become part of it.

We also strongly suggest that they cut all ties with people involved in occult practices or any form of spirituality other than Christianity. If necessary, they should change their email address and phone number. We also emphasize the importance of good company in general. Unfortunately, there are times when the recipient undoes all the work that has been done, for example, by returning to drug use or engaging in immorality. The Bible says that we reap what we sow (Gal 6:8). Our Heavenly Father may consider someone righteous by looking at them through the pure life of Jesus to which this sinner has united by faith. But if a believer constantly falls back into their old sins, it is quite possible that the curses related to disobedience will be reactivated. They will then need to restart the entire deliverance process. Jesus defeated Satan on the cross, but one must ardently desire to be liberated. Lastly, we ask the recipients to repay any debt owed to friends who have been involved in sorcery or the New Age[139]. Similarly, it is important to dispose of all material

---

139 According to some deliverance ministers, a debt can serve as an entry point. It is important to note that this situation is different from financial transactions with a sorcerer, medium, or any other person for the purpose of obtaining occult services. These transactions are clearly agreements with the work of the evil one, which we must cancel through prayer.

related to occult practices, even if they have great monetary or sentimental value because they are inherited from ancestors. We insist that the recipients do not give away these objects (jewelry, books, CDs, totems, pyramids, statues, talismans, etc.), but rather destroy them or throw them away (Acts 19:19).

But how far should such a process go? Some people recommend discarding anything given by someone actively practicing the occult: gifts, clothing, household items (like a vacuum cleaner or a toaster). According to them, these objects could serve as a point of contact to influence the recipient. Another school of thought advocates, on the contrary, simply purifying these common objects by praying over them or using sanctified water. The idea of simply purifying also finds echoes in certain biblical passages:

> *For every creature of God is good,*
> *and nothing to be refused,*
> *if it be received with thanksgiving:*
> *For it is sanctified by the word of God and prayer.*
> 1 Timothy 4:4-5

> *To the pure all things are pure:*
> *but to them that are defiled and unbelieving is nothing pure;*
> *but even their mind and conscience is defiled.*
> Titus 1:15

Moreover, even authors who advocate for discarding personal belongings never go so far as to recommend burning down the houses where the recipients lived with practitioners of occultism. Instead, they advise simply purifying the place as one would for any new dwelling. Is there not a contradiction here?

Unfortunately, I do not believe we can establish a rule that is always valid in this context. I have seen situations where gifts were spiritually poisoned, and others where these objects had no hold over the recipient. Therefore, I think we must make a decision according to what the Spirit dictates, proceed with a clear conscience, and then observe what happens after our actions. It will always be possible to discard things later if we did not do so initially and oppressions continue to manifest after our purification prayers. One thing is certain: we should not keep objects used for occult practices, not even as mementos of the person who used them. The notion of purification applies only to non-specifically occult objects that have been shared with individuals who made pacts with the world of darkness.

Preventive separation

Over the years, we have adopted a practice that facilitates inner healing prayer. We systematically pray for all those we assist during the first or second meeting to separate them from their ancestors. We have observed that this prayer clears the atmosphere around the person being helped, making it easier for them to connect with Jesus and receive revelations from the Spirit. The prayer of separation from ancestors only concerns negative inheritances. We do not want the person being helped to be deprived of the blessings attached to their family. We simply declare that we cut off the negative ties from the maternal and paternal lines, on physical, mental, emotional, sexual, spiritual, and socioeconomic levels. While praying, we listen to God and sometimes declare specific points that we believe we perceive. That is why we generally do not address both parental lines at once.

If more specific generational ties are detected later during our meetings, we will pray again for those particular areas. Indeed, this preventive prayer alone is only partially effective. We can compare it to a cannonball fired on a battlefield. The shot is not very precise, but it generally hits targets; and it allows us to advance more easily afterward. Another comparison we use with those we assist is that of onion layers. Our goal is to gradually remove various layers to discern the core of the problem.

It should be noted that this prayer works whether the person being helped understands our language or not. For example, during a mission trip to Brazil in the fall of 2014, I was one of the trainees praying for people during an evangelization and healing campaign organized by Global Awakening. The collective anointing in the stadium, where thousands had gathered, was wonderful. Some people who came forward to ask for healing had visible pains or deformities, making it easy to verify the results of our prayers. However, sometimes the reason for the prayer request was not visible, and I did not have a translator. In such cases, I prayed in French to separate these individuals from their ancestors and to cast out evil spirits, knowing that there had been much witchcraft in that country. I then prayed for physical healing, and many people indicated that they were touched by God's power at that moment. I believe that many of these ailments were the result of generational ties or evil spirits. What is marvelous is that my language was understood in the heavenly realm, even if it was not understood by the people being helped.

There you have it! I hope this presentation of the concrete steps involved in praying for generational ties will help you navigate this complex reality more effectively. I am not saying that all those you assist will be delivered from all their problems. This is true for any type of intervention, whether secular or religious. Many factors come into play in healing, and God remains sovereign. Moreover, we do not always understand why one person is healed and not another. Additionally, some healings are more gradual than others.

Despite this, we regularly observe that people feel much better after our prayers[140], and we can rejoice in seeing many lives completely transformed. We particularly celebrate the effectiveness of prayers to break generational ties, especially when other methods to bring healing to desperate individuals have failed.

---

140 See the results of a survey conducted among those we assist in my book *Espoir pour l'âme et l'esprit, le miracle de la guérison intérieure.*

Conclusion

Reflecting on the truths contained in the Word of God regarding generational inheritances, I understood that they are similar to the mechanism by which we inherit original sin, aligning with a fundamental truth stated in Romans 5:12-14: each person is judged for their own sins, but we can all inherit the consequences of our ancestors' wrong actions. This principle expressed by the Apostle Paul does not align with the federalist explanation of original sin. Contrary to what this theology explains, the Bible tells us that we did not inherit the guilt of Adam and Eve, but rather we received from them the tendency to sin and the consequences of their sin, which affect our health, family life, work environment, and all of creation.

The idea that we inherit consequences and not guilt is also mentioned in the Law (Deut 5:9 and 24:16) and by the prophet Jeremiah (Jer 32:18-19). Conditional covenants, like the Mosaic covenant, also describe the curses that befall the descendants of those who disobey God's commandments (Deut 28:15-68). These texts demonstrate that the notion of generational ties is the family-level counterpart of the mechanics of original sin. Moreover, by reading in their contexts the popular proverbs of sour grapes cited in Ezekiel 18:2 and Jeremiah 31:29, we understand that these passages do not contradict the notion of generational ties. In fact, once we understand the principle of the transmission of curses and not guilt, everything becomes so clear. We are guilty of our individual sins, but not of our fathers' iniquity. However, the lives of ancestors have consequences for their descendants, which can create generational ties.

Before embarking on writing this book, I had never read any authors who connected generational ties to original sin. However, after finishing this work, someone brought to my attention an online document authored by Dr. Arlin Epperson. This man has a deliverance ministry and teaches on this subject. He arrived at the same conclusions as I did:

> Adam and Eve committed what is generally called original sin. Therefore, all the children born to them (and their descendants) inherited sin as a spiritual gene, thereby turning original sin into hereditary sin. Subsequently, the whole human race has had the same sinful nature; also, the curse of rejection and the penalty of spiritual death has been passed down through the process of conception and birth (Rom. 5:12)[141].
>
> Exodus 20:5 uses the word iniquity. There is much confusion about the difference that exists between the terms sin and iniquity. There are 16 Greek & Hebrew words that are translated into English as "iniquity". In some scripture verses, it means "gross sin". In this scripture reference it means the effect or consequences of sin on others. Simply put, sin is the cause, and the iniquity is the result of the sin on others. Ezek 18 makes it very plain that children are not responsible for the sins of their parents. However, if a parent commits a sin (such as occult involvement or sexual sin), it produces a curse. The parent committed the sin, but the curse causes a generational iniquity or weakness which is passed down within the family line[142].

We also discussed demons. Original sin began with the intervention of the devil. Humans allied with him and ceded domination of the world to him. The activity of demons has not ceased since. Sins, traumas, and witchcraft not only open the door to curses but also to evil spirits, which sometimes are passed down from generation to generation in certain families, exacerbating

---

141 [On line] Epperson (Arlin), "Healing of the Spirit – A practical manual for Delivrance and Inner Healing", Version 7, MI/É.-U., 2014, p. 119. http://www.healingofthespirit.org/wp-content/uploads/2016/01/Healing-of-the-Spirit-Chapters-1-32.pdf (Sept 22, 2022).

142 *Ibid*, p. 59.

mentalities and afflicting people. Fortunately for us, God had a plan from the beginning. Jesus came to destroy the works of the devil.

God made Himself known by first proposing the covenants of the Old Testament. Through them, He clarified what is good and evil to reveal the nature of sin. But these conditional covenants were not kept. That is why God established a superior covenant directly between Himself and His Son. By the Holy Spirit, this covenant has the power to perfectly deliver from evil, educate, and transform the hearts of born-again believers. All previous covenants, both conditional and unconditional, converged toward this New Covenant in Jesus Christ. The New Testament now proclaims the effectiveness of the Cross: it can counter all the ills that humanity suffers, including negative generational inheritances. Healing and life can now extend into all the painful cracks of the past and regenerate the tree of life of our families. This is also affirmed by Epperson.

> Exodus 20:5 informs us, "[…] visiting the iniquity of the fathers upon the children unto the third and fourth generation of them that hate me." Within this scripture, the children did not sin – but the consequences of their father's sin follow them through a generational curse until the original sin(s) are repented of and covered by the blood of Jesus. [...] Jesus took upon himself our sins and died on the cross for us that we might be made free[143].

> Let there be no mistake, the forgiveness of our sins has already been provided for by the death of Jesus on the cross. We are not accountable for the sins of previous generations, but God did not promise we would also escape the consequences of their sins without divine intervention[144].

---

143 *Ibid*, p. 213.
144 *Ibid,* p. 60.

The restoration of all things mentioned in the New Covenant and the definitive disappearance of evil will only occur at the end of times when Jesus returns. However, we can already experience some of the power of the world to come. Upon our conversion, our status before God changes instantly. We are adopted as children of God and reconciled. We receive the Spirit as a guarantee of our future inheritance. Nothing can take this salvation from us, not even demons (Rom 8:38-39). Furthermore, we can obtain other benefits from Christ's propitiation in all areas where humanity has been weakened. However, it is essential to understand that sanctification, healing, and deliverance from evil spirits or generational ties are not automatically acquired at the moment of conversion. All these things are accessible only to those who ask for them with faith.

The reality of generational ties and spirits is depicted in the Bible, described in the history of the Church, and conveyed by the testimony of many Christians even today. The presence of such ties often explains the failure of conventional healing approaches. Fortunately, the Lord has not left His Church without resources. It is on the basis of the Cross that we pray. And, although in practice it is not always easy to discern the origin of evil buried in the distant past of previous generations, the mystery of iniquity can still be unveiled by the Spirit of God who guides us by giving us the necessary discernment. We thus discover which doors were opened in the lives of our ancestors through traumas, sins, and words of cursing. Among these ancestral sins, idolatrous and occult practices particularly bring curses to the descendants, as stated in the second commandment (Ex 20:5-6 and Deut 5:9-10), which is still valid. Satan binds the posterity of those who make pacts with him. But the Cross can save those who say, "Father, deliver us from the evil one."

The Lord Jesus is the great victor. He has desired to give us the keys so that we may fight in His name. He has given us the authority to bind sins, free believers from the snares of the devil, and break the ties that paralyze them so that they may be released into their destinies. Though the Church's fight is noble, it is not always easy. Humans are complex, and the spiritual world is filled with mysteries. I believe the Lord likes to remind us that He answers us not according to a user's manual, but purely by grace.

The theme of generational ties has been little explored by theologians until now. This book, I hope, has helped to clear some ground. However, it would be desirable for various researchers to deepen our biblical knowledge on the prayer of healing, particularly regarding generational ties. I am still delighted to be able to help pastors, secular workers, and the general public better understand the notion of generational ties. Additionally, I would be pleased if some of you felt inspired to continue your practitioner training by reading the manual I have produced[145]. Many captives are waiting for us to deliver them from evil, with God's help, in the name of Jesus. May God bless and accompany you!

---

145 Robillard (Michel), *La prière de guérison intérieure – Manuel de formation*, Québec, 2022, 245 p.

Bibliography

Articles

Décarie (S.), "Adolescente et enceinte, quand l'échec contraceptif mène à la pauvreté", L'omnipraticien, April 1994.

Genuis (S.J.), "The Dilemma of Adolescent Sexuality, Part III- Teenage Pregnancy", Journal SOGC, January 1994.

Scott (David), "Pornography: Its Effects on the Family, Community, and Culture", Washington [DC], The Child and Family Protection Institutes, 1985.

Sylvester (C.), "Preventable Calamity", Progressive Policy Institute, 1994.

Conferences

Anderson (Shannae), Hutchkin (Mike), Fish (Ken), *Healing Generational Trauma Conference*, six videos from an online conference, January 22-23, 2021.

Books

Allen (Michael), *Karl Barth's Church Dogmatics – An Introduction and Reader*, London et New-York, T & T Clarck, 2012, 241 p.

Bloesh (Donald G.), *The Struggle of Prayer*, Colorado Springs [CO], Helmers & Howard, 1988, 415 p.

Clark (Randy), *The Biblical Guidebook to Deliverance,* Lake Mary [FL], Charisma House, 2015, 190 p.

Djaballhah (Amar), *Paraboles aujourd'hui,* Québec, La Clairière, 1994, 343 p.

Fee (Gordon), *God's Empowering Presence – The Holy Spirit in the Letters of Paul*, Grand Rapids [MI], Baker Academics, 1994, 967 p.

Grudem (Wayne), *Théologie systématique*, Charols [France], Éditions Excelsis, 2010, 1493 p.

Hammond (Frank et Ida Mae), *Les voleurs dans le temple*, Pomy [Suisse], Soteria, 1992, 250 p.

Hayford (Jack), *Penetrating the Darkness*, Grand Rapids [MI], Chosen books, 2011, 188 p.

Hinn (Benny), *Le sang de l'alliance*, Nîmes, Vida, 1999, 155 p.

Hodge (Charles), *Systematic Theology,* Vol. 2, [s.l.], Hendrickson Publishers, 2003, 732 p.

Horrobin (Peter J.), *Healing through Delivrance*, Grand Rapids [MI], Chosen, 2008, 578 p.

Horton (Stanley M.) *Systematic Theology,* Springfield [MI], Gospel Publishing House, 2000, 704 p.

Lizotte (Michel), *L'homosexualité, les mythes et les faits*, Montréal, Les productions ML, 2008, 305 p.

Lovelace (Richard F.), *Dynamics of Spiritual Life*, Downers Grove [IL], Intervarsity Press, 1979, 455 p.

MacNutt (Francis), *Deliverance from Evil Spirits*, Grand Rapids [MI], Chose-Baker, 2009, 304 p.

Maloney (James), *Living Above the Snake Line*, Bloomington [IN], WestBow Press, 2015, 158 p.

Oden (Thomas C.), *John Wesley's Teachings,* Vol. 1, Grand Rapids [MI], Zondervan, 2012, 240 p.

Olson (Paul), *How to Touch a Leper,* Mound [MN], New Day Publishing Company, 1986, 151 p.

Payne (Leanne), *Crise de la masculinité*, Palézieux [Suisse], Éditions Raphaël, 1994, 138 p.

Payne (Leanne), *Restoring the Christian Soul through healing prayer*, Wheaton [IL], Crossway Books, 1991, 249 p.

Pearlman (Myer), *Knowing the Doctrines of the Bible*, Springfield [MI], Gospel Publishing House, 2018, 397 p.

Pierce (R.W.), Groothuis (R.M.), Fee (G.D.), *Discovering Biblical Equality*, Downers Grove [IL], InterVarsity Press, 2005, 528 p.

Prince (Derek), *Blessing or Curse: You Can Choose*, Grand Rapids [MI], Chosen Books, 1990, 304 p.

Prince (Derek), *Pulling Down Strongholds*, New Kensington [PA], Whitaker House, 2013, 118 p.

Robillard (Michel), *Espoir pour l'âme et l'esprit, le miracle de la guérison intérieure,* Québec, 2022, 124 p.

Robillard (Michel), *La prière de guérison intérieure – Manuel de formation*, Québec, 2022, 245 p.

Sandford (John & Paula), *The Elijah Task*, Tulsa [OK], Victory House, 1977, 239 p.

Reference Works

Barclay (William), *The New Daily Study Bible – The Letters to the Romans*, London, Westminster John Knox Press, 2002, 262 p.

Bromiley (Geoffrey W.), *Theological Dictionnary of the New Testament*, Grand Rapids [MI], Eerdmans Publishing Company, 1985, 1356 p.

Gaebelein (Frank E), *The Expositor's Bible Commentary,* Grand Rapids [MI], collection CDs, Zondervan Publishing House, 1981, 1356 p.

Le Grand Dictionnaire de la Bible, Charols [France], Excelsis, 2004, 1777 p.

Electronic ressources

http://atilf.atilf.fr/dendien/scripts/tlfiv5/advanced.exe?8;s=3810307920 (August 2020).

http://www.cosmovisions.com/Traducianisme.htm (June 27, 2021).

https://www.editions-menor.com/fr/livres/34-faire-face-aux-esprits-familiers.html (August 2020).

http://fiohnetwork.org/?p=1620 (November 2020).

https://florentvarak.toutpoursagloire.com/faut-il-briser-les-liens-dheredite-episode-191/ (July 2020).

https://fr.wikipedia.org/wiki/Familier_(spirit) (August 2020).

https://www.gotquestions.org/Francais/esprits-familiers.html (August 2020).

https://www.iltaime.com/single-post/2018/04/30/LES-LIENS-ANCESTRAUX (August 2020).

https://www.lasaintete.com/etude-biblique-du-mardi-15-mars-2016-invoquer-les-esprits-de-morts-les-esprits-familiers/ (August 2020).

https://liturgie.catholique.fr/accueil/initiation-chretienne/le-bapteme/bapteme-des-petits-enfants/13303-lexorcisme-dans-le-rite-baptismal/ (August 2020).

https://ne-np.facebook.com/DemonologieEtRelationDAide/posts/422673197765820/ (January 2021).

"Epigenetics", Futura Santé, https://www.futura-sciences.com/sante/definitions/genetique-epigenetique-136/ (May 5, 2021).

Epperson (Arlin), "Healing of the Spirit - A practical manual for Deliverance and Inner Healing," Version 7, MI/USA, 2014, 263 p. http://www.healingofthespirit.org/wp-content/uploads/2016/01/Healing-of-the-Spirit-Chapters-1-32.pdf (September 22, 2022).

Geddes (Linda), "Fear of a smell can be passed down several generations," December 1, 2013, https://www.newscientist.com/article/dn24677-fear-of-a-smell-can-be-passed-down-several-generations/#ixzz6xcUqwcag (June 12, 2021).

Lanel (Yves), https://www.youtube.com/watch?v=yld0Q-OaxYc (September 30, 2020).

Lewis (Tanya), "Fearful Experiences Passed On In Mouse Families," December 5, 2013, https://www.livescience.com/41717-mice-inherit-fear-scents-genes.html (June 12, 2021).

"Pastor John Piper Answers You," https://www.reveniralevangile.com/ma-vie-peut-elle-etre-marquee-par-des-peches-des-sorts-ou-des-maledictions-generationnels/ (July 2020).

Søndergaard (Torben), https://www.youtube.com/watch?v=p55AMpE9jkA (September 30, 2020).

Trescases (Nathalie), Thorin (Eric), "Epigenetics? Jamais entendu parler..." (April 11, 2017).

https://observatoireprevention.org/2017/04/11/epigenetique-jamais-entenu-parler/ (May 5, 2021).

For more information : eva-quebec.com/pgi

To contact the author : mrlepcac@gmail.com

www.ingramcontent.com/pod-product-compliance
Lightning Source LLC
LaVergne TN
LVHW050023080526
838202LV00069B/6893